D0367174

I Wish
I Could Say
I Love
You

CHOICE BOOKS
The Best In Family Reading
P. O. Box 503
Goshen, IN 46526
"We Welcome Your Response"

Muriel Canfield

I Wish
I Could Say
I Love
you

BETHANY HOUSE PUBLISHERS
MINNEAPOLIS, MINNESOTA 55438
A Division of Bethany Fellowship, Inc.

Certain names and events in this book have been changed or altered.

Scripture quotations designated (GNB) are from the *Good News Bible*, the Bible in Today's English Version. Copyright © American Bible Society, 1976.

Text excerpts from pages xii, 139, 140, and 191 from *The Navy Wife*, Third Revised Edition, by Anne Briscoe Pye and Nancy Shea. Copyright, 1942, 1945, 1949, 1955, by Harper & Row, Publishers, Inc. By permission of the publisher.

Published by Bethany House Publishers
A Division of Bethany Fellowship, Inc.
6820 Auto Club Road, Minneapolis, Minnesota 55438

Printed in the United States of America

Library of Congress Cataloging in Publication Data

Canfield, Muriel, 1935-
    I wish I could say I love you.

    1. Canfeld, Muriel, 1935-   . 2. Converts—United States—Biography. 3. Alcoholics—United Stated—Biography. I. Title.
BV4935.C26A38 1983   248.2'5'0924 [B]   82-24486
ISBN 0-87123-265-0

*Dedicated
to Gene*

ABOUT THE AUTHOR

MURIEL CANFIELD was born in Oak Park, Illinois, and raised in suburban Chicago. She married in 1956 and has three children. She and her husband were converted to Christ after 17 years of marriage. She has been a full-time writer for the past three years. She has a degree in Education from Miami University.

PREFACE

At the age of fourteen, I left my church, my minister, and my God—more exactly, my conception of God. I was sure that if God existed, He was just like my minister, the Reverend Dr. Kinder, who peered through steel-rimmed glasses, rarely smiled, and preached in solemn tones with long, flat O's and A's. The Reverend Dr. Kinder and, therefore, God depressed me. I was one who liked fun, and I wanted love. I was certain that God did not offer either of these.

The day I left God I did not know that I would drink thousands of bottles of beer and hundreds of bottles of bourbon before I came back to Him. While I drank those bottles, there were few moments of fun, and very little love. Mostly it was hell.

CHAPTER I

I awoke, opened my eyes and winced, feeling as if a car had rolled over me and crushed my head. Stretching up, I reached through a slat of gray moonlight and turned on the bedside lamp. It was 9:00 p.m. Except for the ticking of the clock and the dripping of water from the bathroom faucet, the house was quiet. Apparently my husband, Gene, and my children were still driving back from Minneapolis, thank heaven. But as I was thanking my luck, the full impact of what I had done crushed in upon me and I started to cry. I despised myself. But I didn't have time to sit and cry. If I hurried, I could clean up the house, take a shower, brush my teeth—and Gene would think I had spent the weekend nursing my flu, as I had said I would.

I moved from the bed and carefully bent over to pick up the Seagram's bottle under the night table, the overflowing ashtray beside my shoe, the two white coffee mugs that held the dregs of the coffee-bourbon mix. In a minute I would come back for the pizza box and the stale slice of pizza on the floor.

In the kitchen, when I set the ashtray in the sink, I saw a note at the end of the counter near the stove. Gene's upright, squeezed handwriting, the writing as contained as Gene himself, stared back at me. Trembling, I reached for it. I knew that it would be telling me he had come in, taken one look, and left—for good.

If only I hadn't gotten drunk, I thought, *this weekend wouldn't have happened.* But then, a moment of truth and I understood that from the beginning I had been heading like an arrow for this day—drinking and not loving Gene.

I remembered the beginning.

September, mid-fifties.

Gravel crunched under our spiked heels as Lisa and I saun-
tered across the parking lot fronting Freddie's, a grayed-out
frame tavern next to the railroad tracks in Bellwood, Illinois.
My pencil-slim skirt and a blue cashmere sweater tucked under the skirt waist and held in with a wide, black belt were the
height of fashion, and I tossed my curls back with perky confidence. I looked quite pretty, I hoped, because in Freddie's I
would be celebrating my second-to-last day as Muriel Hansen.
On Friday I would become Mrs. Eugene Canfield. Earlier I
had explained to Gene that tonight Lisa and I would shop at
Marshall Field, then eat a pizza and see a film. The lie was a
necessity; for Gene, a conservative person who did not fre-
quent bars, would not have approved of this celebration.

I bent to run my fingers along my stocking seams, while
Lisa impatiently tapped her toe against the gravel.

"They're already straight," she said. Lisa was always in a
rush.

"I'm coming, I'm coming," I said.

"Hi," I called to Freddie over Lisa's shoulder as we entered.

Freddie's wave was nonchalant. "Hi, girls." A pause, then,
"Two old-fashioneds with two cherries?"

"Yes," we said. I smiled at Freddie, appreciating his mem-
ory.

We hiked up onto stools at the long, curving bar. The air
was thick with smoke, the bitter smell of beer, the beat of
jukebox jazz.

"What time is it?" I asked Lisa.

"I don't know," she said hurriedly and turned, not to me
but to a man on her left who was asking, "Can I buy you that
drink?"

"Fine," Lisa said.

I lighted a cigarette and watched the smoke wind toward
the ceiling, then glanced around. A couple of stools away to
the right a thin young man with a pointed chin, a beaklike
nose, and a mass of slicked-down black hair dragged at a cigarette. On the stool beside him a wizened man hunched over his
drink. At the end of the bar a young couple huddled close.
Nobody here of much interest, I thought, while Freddie placed
my old-fashioned on the bar. Since Lisa already was occupied

and I was determined to celebrate, I leaned over the empty stool and said to the man with the black hair, "Have you ever seen Freddie out from behind the bar?"

He snorted, then laughed. "Never! Freddie's always in there." He swept his eyes over me in appraisal, taking in my snug skirt, slim waist, soft sweater. He studied my eyes. "Blue's my favorite color," he said. "Like some company?"

"Sure."

While he moved to the adjacent stool, I imagined the fit Gene would have if he knew I was here. Gene would never think of doing such a thing. Mom often said, "He's a fine young man," and Dad said, "He's got his head screwed on straight."

Gene thought I shared his system of ethics; I wanted to and I planned to, but not tonight. I had to have this last night for me, because I didn't love Gene.

I took a sip from the old-fashioned, and the black-haired man leaned close and said, "I've never seen you here before."

"I come sometimes."

"Do you live in Bellwood?"

"No, in Elmhurst."

"A pretty ritzy place."

"It's okay." With Gene still strongly in my mind I added, "I think some people set their standards too high. A person's got to be human."

"Right," he said.

"Gene's got his too high."

"Who's Gene?"

"A friend—a boyfriend, I guess."

"Serious?"

"No, not really."

Evidently pleased about that, the black-haired man laughed. "Like another drink, honey?" he asked.

"Yes."

He signaled Freddie with his finger. We had the drink—and many more, until my head became foamy and the barroom took on a splendor and the black-haired man became a fine person, a friend. I murmured, "Gene thinks I drink too much sometimes. He made me promise I'd drink only three drinks a night, but not until two days from now. Tonight it's okay to drink more."

"What right's he got to tell you how much to drink?"

I paused to give that some thought. "None. When you think about it, it's none of his business." I dropped my voice confidentially, "It's Gene's fault I'm quitting college." I was lying, but right then it seemed to be entirely Gene's fault.

The black-haired man's eyes held disinterest. "Don't you want to hear?" I challenged.

"Shoot," he said.

"I can't say," I said, suddenly morose. "It's too sad." And I almost cried as I thought about my clipped-off senior year and my clipped-off degree in English education and my hasty decision last week to marry Gene and not finish college. But what else could I have done? My junior year had been a two-semester stretch of drinking parties with little studying in between. If I returned to school, I would fail those difficult courses scheduled for next semester.

"Gene did you a favor," he said.

"He did not. I loved college."

"College is for birdbrains," he said and went on to expound on his view of education and self-righteous people.

"I don't like negativism," I inserted into the monologue, depressed by his sour outlook and beginning to think him not so fine, not such a good friend.

I'd had enough of him. "I've got to go. It's late."

"It's not late," he argued, his sharp chin jutting belligerently. "Stay."

Ignoring him, I turned to Lisa and whispered, "Let's go somewhere else."

"I can't. I've got to get home," she said. "I work tomorrow. You too—or did you forget?"

"Nuts." I had forgotten that tomorrow would be Thursday and I would be on the nine-to-five shift at Millie's tobacco and gift shop.

While Lisa wrote out her phone number for her new boy-friend, the black-haired man changed his approach: "Don't go now, honey—things are getting good."

"I told you, I've got to go." I frowned in irritation as I drained my glass, set it on the bar, and slid from the stool.

He grabbed my arm and demanded, "Have another drink."

"Let me go!" I pulled away and stepped back.

"Let's go," I urged Lisa. "He's getting nasty."

Behind Lisa, I wobbled toward the door, followed by the

black-haired man's curses.

"Can you drive?" Lisa wondered aloud.

"Of course." But my head spun and the door wavered. "I'm just fine," I assured her.

I poked along in Dad's Packard toward Elmhurst. When drunk, I always drove five or ten miles under the speed limit.

"Can't you speed it up?" Lisa asked, impatient again.

"Do you want me to wreck my dad's car?"

"No."

"Then relax," I said. "Did I tell you that after I'm married, I can't drink more than three drinks a night? Gene made me promise."

"Sneak them," was Lisa's advice.

"Maybe," I said as we inched around a corner. "But maybe three's enough. Three's a lot, you know." Lisa's shrug was noncommittal.

Three drinks would do for me, but they sure wouldn't do for my parents; to them three was just a start. In my childhood, as now, Mom and Dad had been periodic drinkers, drinking around-the-clock for five or six weeks, then sobering up for five or six weeks. But even when drunk, they had been kind and loving to my sisters and me and had often taken us along to the taverns.

I liked best going to the Dewdrop Inn. Dad would put Mom, my sisters Chris and Ellen, and me in his Packard; then instead of driving to the Dewdrop Inn via St. Charles Road, we veered into the quarter-mile field next to our house. "Hold on!" he yelled every few hundred feet. "Keep your hat on!"

"Watch out!" my sisters and I shouted in high excitement each time we neared a tree.

At the Dewdrop Inn while Dad and Mom drank shots of bourbon chased with water, my sisters and I put nickels in the slot machine, played cards, and giggled at the sign on the ceiling: "What are you looking up here for?"

"Don't look up," we said to each other, but we always did.

Some of the men at the bar fussed over us, saying that we were pretty and sweet and that we had lovely hair. These comments made me feel uncomfortable. But Francie, the owner's wife, an immense woman, always gave us sweet looks. And she fried us hamburgers and poured all the Cokes we wanted.

When it was time to leave, we got into the Packard and bounced back through the field. At home Mom and Dad continued drinking, either at the kitchen table or in bed. As a child, I considered taverns, kitchen tables, and beds as normal places for drinking.

Though my parents were kind, I yearned for a sober mom and dad and swore I would never drink like them. Yet here I was . . .

Lisa broke into my reverie. "Muriel, you've sat through a green light."

I slammed down the gas pedal and the car leaped into the intersection.

"Not now!" Lisa screamed. "The light's red!"

I jammed on the brakes, glanced into the rearview mirror—clear—and backed up. "Nuts," I said in apology. "I was thinking. I've decided not to drink after I'm married. I mean it. Tonight at Freddie's I had my last. I'm not going to be like my parents."

When the light switched to green, I cruised across the intersection and on down St. Charles Road.

"Turn," Lisa commanded. We were at her street, lined with huge homes separated from each other by immaculate lawns.

I turned and said, "If Gene knew where I'd been tonight, he'd pass out."

"Look, going to Freddie's was your idea, not mine. I didn't drag you there," Lisa said as I pulled up to her house.

"I didn't say you did." She reached for the door.

"See you at the wedding," I said as she climbed from the car.

"See you."

"I wasn't accusing you of anything," I called after her, because I hated to have any ill will between anyone and me. I liked peace, a smooth world with no fights.

"Okay," she called over her shoulder.

I drove slowly back past the large houses, the high school, then across the railroad tracks. Just beyond the tracks I came to our narrow frame house with its flaking paint and worn hardwood floors that shook each time a train rumbled by. If only I lived on Lisa's side of the tracks, I thought, then turned into the drive, passed between the hawthorn tree and Dad's West Suburban Roofing Company sign, and parked before the garage where he stored his shingles. I hurried upstairs and was asleep moments after I got into bed.

Gene called me the next morning at Millie's. "How was the movie and pizza?"

"They were good. We had cheese and pepperoni." This would be the last lie between Gene and me, because I wouldn't be drinking again. At least, I decided in a flash, from now on I'd *seldom* drink. I would not exclude festive occasions, that is, very festive occasions, ones where it would appear odd to abstain—such as weddings.

"I missed you," Gene said.

"Weren't you with Dan and Bill and Gene Anderson?"

"Yes, but the whole time I wished I were with you."

"I wished I were with you too." Another lie, but only a small one.

"Can you come to dinner tonight? My parents want you to meet a couple of aunts."

"Okay."

"Till then, darling," he said. "I love you."

"See you tonight," I responded.

Later at the Canfields', Mr. Canfield, always an affectionate man, greeted me with an enthusiastic hug. Though Gene was quiet, his father was not. He loved to talk—to lean back in his recliner and spin stories of his country youth.

Mr. Canfield led me into the living room. "Have a seat," he invited. "Gene's not here yet, but he should be back in five or ten minutes." Introductions to the two aunts followed.

I realized that I was hugging my purse like a pillow, as I did when I was nervous and feeling insecure and wanting others to like me. I set the purse down beside my chair.

Aunt Sarah leaned forward. "Are you excited about the wedding?" she inquired and continued without a pause. "Where will you live, downtown or out here? Is Gene still working for that place near the Loop—?"

"Yes," I broke in. "It's Harza Engineering Company."

"You'll live downtown?"

"No, at my parents' cottage on Lake Michigan." Two pairs of eyes waited expectantly. "We don't have a place here yet." Aunt Sarah and Aunt Elsie nodded, which I took as a signal to continue. "We'll be looking soon." They nodded again. "The wedding's tomorrow, you know."

"We know," said Aunt Sarah, smiling at Aunt Elsie.

"Your wedding was so lovely," said Aunt Sarah, turning to Aunt Elsie. "Remember? Mother served those little sandwiches—"

"Hors d'oeuvres," interrupted Aunt Elsie. "She made them with chicken and egg salad."

"I didn't have hors d'oeuvres," retorted Aunt Elsie firmly. "I had cold cuts—turkey and ham."

It turned out that the hors d'oeuvres had been served at Cousin Nancy's wedding reception; and further, they remembered, Cousin Nancy had had a three-tiered cake.

To me it was as if they spoke a foreign language, for weddings in my family were not a matter of hors d'oeuvres or cold cuts or cake. At a Hansen wedding my father drank far too much and said (again and again), "During the Depression Old Henry and I sold sewing machines and slept under bridges and ate peanut butter sandwiches." And Mom, also into the drinks, sniffled that no one loved her and that no one ever would and that all her life she would be friendless.

Gene's mother taught Sunday school, his father was an accountant; they both attended church, rarely missing a Sunday. We Hansens never went to churches or anyplace besides the taverns. *Gene's mother and father are such regular people,* I thought.

About that time Gene walked in, a gray suit on his six-foot frame, carrying a briefcase. *Dad has never carried a briefcase,* I thought as Gene leaned over and kissed the top of my head. "Darling," he whispered, so that the aunts would not hear.

Hours later, after chicken and dumplings, a few country stories by Mr. Canfield, and more reminiscing from the aunts, we got into Gene's Chevrolet. In his careful way, Gene kept the car below the speed limit; he did not believe in breaking the law. In contrast, when I was sober I would drive the highways at 80 or 90, enjoying the free feeling of the speed.

"You'll kill us," Gene would scold when he was my passenger. Though put off by my boldness, he also delighted in it. "You make me feel happy," he would tell me, viewing me as a joyful free spirit. He didn't know of my insecurity, thinking my excessive drinking came from an impetuous nature. I had promised to cut back and he thought I would. He was like the painter who loved the woman on his canvas, and I usually chose behavior that would confirm his picture of me.

I wondered if my mental "painting" of Gene reflected the real person. He held himself erect, carrying a calm manner on a tall frame. Large bones, broad shoulders, and hard muscles in his arms and legs gave me a sense of his strength and ability. His hair was brown, his eyes pale blue. His face was not particularly handsome but attractive in a rough kind of way.

Above all, he was intelligent.

With all those credentials, I knew I should love him. I *wanted* to love him. But he seemed so quiet and rather dull. I really was looking for someone more flamboyant, like me. But Gene was the best of the men I knew, and I felt I must get married.

We were at the St. Charles Road intersection and a collie darted in front of the car. He braked hard and snapped, "Stupid, idiot mutts!"

"I like dogs."

"I hate them!"

"Your folks have one."

"They shouldn't."

"I'd like one after we're married."

He smiled and I knew that if I insisted, he would buy me a dog.

I thought again about our dissimilar families. "Your parents are pretty religious," I remarked.

"They've always been like that."

"Does it bother you?"

"No."

"Why aren't you religious?" I asked.

"I just don't like church."

"Why not?"

Because he was contemplative, Gene paused a moment before answering, then said, "My parents belonged to four or five churches and—"

"What's that got to do with not liking church?" I interrupted.

"I heard too many doctrines. Every church thinks it's got the answer."

"So?"

"So, which one's got it?"

"You're turned off."

"Completely."

"I'm turned off, too," I admitted, remembering the day I had left church and the Reverend Dr. Kinder and God. "Do you believe in God?" I asked.

"Not really. He might exist, but I don't think so."

"Sometimes I pray."

"Then you believe in God?"

"I don't know. It seems like I'm praying to the air."

"You probably are, but what's the difference. If God's around, He's around. If He's not, He's not."

I liked the way Gene had expressed that. "Right. If He's here, He's here."

Gene shrugged, glanced from the road to me, and patted the seat. "Come on over, gal."

I moved close to him and he brushed my hair with his lips and said, "I love you."

"Hmmm."

"Tomorrow you'll be mine forever."

"I know."

We turned into my parents' driveway. Gene parked and pulled me into his arms. "I can't tell you how much I love you, darling."

"Neither can I." I lifted my head from his chest. "But I've got to go. There's a lot to do before tomorrow."

I reached for the door handle. "Not so quick, honey." Gene gathered me in close and kissed me. "Forever, gal," he whispered.

I won't think about forever, I thought, and left him.

Minutes before the wedding, I wanted to rush from our living room and ship out to sea like Ishmael in *Moby Dick*. As did Ishmael, I felt damp and drizzly. *I can't go through with this marriage*, I thought. But how could I cancel it when the caterer was in the kitchen, the presents on the cedar chest, and the fiancé and guests in the living room? I couldn't.

So I married Gene in my living room in front of the piano, watched by the guests and by Richard, my family's Airedale.

The reception began. It flowed from the living room to the dining room to the upstairs family room, all through the house. And rushing from room to room was my Aunt Red, her red hair tumbling lower and lower on her forehead, now almost into her eyes, as she drank champagne. Given her speed and her hair, I figured she was probably on her ninth or tenth glass. Aunt Red paused in the family room, sank to the floor, and sang, "I'm better than an orange, better than a carrot . . ."

I stood before her and hummed along while I drank my champagne. From the corner of my eye I saw Dad coming toward us, weaving slightly, but not stumbling. "Stop the singing, Red," he said. Whenever his sister sang, he demanded that she quit.

"It's a good song, Dad," I said.

He listened. "Not bad."

"She's got a good voice."

"Old Henry was quite a singer," Dad said, adding that Henry had sung "Hallelujah, I'm a bum" in the clearest tenor in Chicago. Which reminded Dad that during the Depression he and Henry had eaten peanut butter sandwiches by day and slept under bridges by night. I quickly moved on.

I went downstairs and found Mom in the living room, sitting on the piano bench, her face long, her eyes misty. I hugged her and asked, "Why so sad?"

"You're leaving me."

"No, not really. We won't be far away."

"It won't be the same," she said and sighed, then went to refill her glass.

Although I had drunk seven or eight champagnes, I figured it was my wedding reception, one of those special occasions, and that I should be having fun. Gene would understand. I got up and started up the stairs. Halfway up, I met Gene. "Come on up," I said. "Maybe we can sing."

"I think we ought to be going."

"I don't feel like going. Why should we go?"

"Because I want to be alone with you and"—he studied my face—"I think you've had enough."

"I think I'm okay." I was in better condition than Aunt Red, who might be singing, and Mom, who was probably crying, and Dad, who would be talking about bridges and Henry.

Gene stepped down to my step and kissed me lightly. "Darling, let's go."

"But—"

"It's time for our honeymoon," he urged.

"All right," I sighed and reluctantly followed him from the reception.

CHAPTER II

We spent the two and a half days of our honeymoon in the Chicago Loop in an old, elegant hotel. On the first day while eating lunch in the hotel restaurant, I dropped my fork on the plate and ran from the table to the lobby, gasping for breath and feeling as if I would smother. Gene dashed after me and stood by helplessly while I struggled for, and finally caught, my breath. Despite his urgings, I refused to return to the restaurant. On the second day in the middle of a film, my throat and lungs again tightened. I gasped and ran from the theater with Gene fast behind me. When I caught my breath, he said, "What's wrong, darling?"

"I felt like I was suffocating. I'm afraid to go back in."

"Maybe you should see a doctor."

The next day we moved into my parents' cottage on Lake Michigan, and I immediately called a doctor and told him what had happened. "I'm petrified," I said. "When it happens, I feel as if I'm going to die."

"You're in no danger of dying," he said. He explained that I had marriage nerves; they were not too uncommon and would be gone in no time—just as soon as I adjusted to marriage. As the doctor predicted, the nerves quickly left, but spontaneously, not because I was adjusting to marriage. At all times I felt trapped and several times during the first week at the cottage I thought, *I should have canceled the wedding, and somehow given back the presents and sent the caterer and guests and Gene home.*

But I hadn't. I was stuck in a marriage with a man I didn't love. I had to accept that.

But evidently I couldn't. On the tenth day of our marriage, after buying milk and eggs, I found myself walking into the liquor store at the corner. *I've got to buy a bottle*, I thought. I was a wreck. I was certain those marriage nerves would return. Gene wouldn't mind if I drank. He knew nothing about my plan to drink only on festive occasions; therefore he wouldn't blink when he saw me having the three drinks we'd agreed on.

But as I decided that, I thought about the peace drinks gave, ironing every feeling of insecurity, every worry, every wrinkle in the world. They would give me a happier marriage. And I figured out a scheme that would allow me to keep the agreement, yet have more than three drinks. But to carry it out I would need privacy so that Gene wouldn't think I was cheating on the agreement.

Because our cottage was small, finding a private spot would be difficult. There were two bedrooms without closets, a kitchen about the size of a closet, a combination living-dining room, and a bathroom with a crack running diagonally across the door. Though the crack was wide enough to see through, I decided that the bathroom would be the best bet. The door locked and the room was long enough to hide from anyone looking through the crack. Best of all, at the end of the long wall was a tier of metal shelves filled with Dad's fishing gear. Gene never fished, and it was unlikely he would go through the gear.

I bought a fifth of bourbon and three quarts of beer. At home I put the beer in the refrigerator and laid the bottle on a shelf in the bathroom between a tackle box and the wall. I then carefully covered it with a towel.

That night I poured several ounces of beer into a glass, took the glass to the shelf, lifted out the fifth, and poured in several ounces of bourbon. That night and every night for a couple of weeks, I was able to get high on three "beers" without a word of complaint from Gene—although I caught him giving me puzzled looks.

But one night I forgot to stand by the storage shelves and stood in front of the crack as I spiked my beer. I heard a squeak, a rustle, a tap against the door. I looked up and saw Gene's eye peering through the crack. Flustered at the discovery, I flew into a fury and yelled, "Get away from the door, you sneak! Don't you know a bathroom's absolutely private?"

"Now I know why you get so looped on three beers." His voice was high-pitched with anger. "We agreed to *three* drinks a night."

"We never said what *kind* of drinks. We just said three drinks. They could be anything." I tilted the glass and drank. "Take your eye out of the door and leave me alone."

"Cheater."

"Spy."

"Get out of the bathroom."

"I'm staying. I'm never coming out."

I heard Gene pad from the door into the living room. "Apologize, you spy!" I yelled. "I won't come out until you do."

Instead of an answer, I heard a click and a blast of sound as the television came on. I sank to the floor, leaned against the wall, finished my drink, and started on the bourbon. At some point, I blacked out.

I woke with an aching head, a terrible thirst, and a queasy stomach. A high sun slanted light through the bedroom window and across the bed. It was close to noon. The last thing I could recall was leaning against the bathroom wall with the bottle between my knees, wondering if I should return to Northwestern University and finish my English education degree. I felt up to the fifty-mile drive and the rigorous studies. I couldn't sit around vegetating. In between that thought and now, Gene had gone to work and I had gotten to bed. How? I wondered.

Not via Gene, I hoped. If he had taken me to bed, then he would know I had drunk far more than three spiked beers. He might be furious. Until last night I had believed he had an easygoing, accepting nature—that in any situation he would eventually give me my way. For the most part I still believed that, but his show of anger was unsettling.

I worried all day about the fight that might be coming. When I heard his car, I went to the kitchen window and watched him get out. His hair was standing in unruly curls, as if he had been running his fingers through it. His lips were set in a tight line.

I ran to the bedroom so that he wouldn't see that I was waiting for him. When I saw him putting his briefcase on the couch, I ambled out. "Did you have a good day?" I said.

"I carried you to bed like a sack of potatoes!" he snapped. "I hope you never repeat last night."

"I won't. It was an accident."

"How can that be an accident?"

"I don't know, but it was."

"Impossible," he said.

"I've been nervous. It's hard to be married when you're not used to it. It won't happen again. Really, I'm sorry."

His mouth relaxed and I saw that he was accepting my apology. "I expect that your three drinks will be *unspiked*. I expect that you'll stick to *three*."

"I will. I promise."

I meant to keep my promise, but a couple of nights later I found myself in the bathroom pouring bourbon into my beer.

Though Gene and I fought about it, I continued spiking my beer. I hated the fights, and when confronted, I apologized profusely. Gene always accepted the apology, then I turned around and drank again. It seemed as if we were falling into a pattern, maybe the only pattern available—to Gene, who in his love gave me awesome acceptance, and to me, who had to drink.

About six weeks after we moved to the lake, I got a job as a laboratory technician. I would be training to co-manage a five-person chemical laboratory. I enjoyed the lab work, but abhorred the training program, which included much chemistry that I didn't understand. I hadn't studied chemistry since my senior year in high school and was sure that my boss had mistakenly hired me.

One night over dinner, I told Gene. "I'm scared to death. I don't understand half of what my boss says. He knows it and I know he's getting ready to fire me."

"He hired you. He must think you can do it."

"Maybe he misread my application."

"You can do it. He doesn't expect you to know everything at once. Give yourself time."

"Should I quit?"

"Aren't you listening? You'll do fine."

About that time Gene applied for the Navy's Officer Candidate School in Newport, Rhode Island. Often I would find myself thinking, *Please, please let him be accepted so that I can leave this lab.* I didn't know if my thoughts were directed to fate, the Navy, or God.

But the thoughts were answered; on the four-month anniversary of our marrige Gene received news that he had been accepted. I immediately quit my job and he left for Newport. I joined him a few weeks later.

Shortly after my arrival I became pregnant.

Gene and I were pleased. In my pleasure my misgivings about marrying Gene were replaced by such a great affection for him that I almost forgot that I didn't love him. I now desired to be a fine wife. It seemed natural for a future mother to desire that. It also seemed natural not to drink, and I stopped without giving it a thought. Without the fights over the drinks, our marrige improved and we were reasonably happy as we waited for the baby.

To prepare for the day when Gene would be commissioned and I would be the wife of an ensign in the United States Navy, I read *The Navy Wife* by Pye and Shea. In it I learned that I would be expected to adhere to correct etiquette, to develop "social graces," such as bridge, dancing, and golf,[1] and to become a "loving, loyal, and competent wife." Pye and Shea wrote: "There is not a shadow of a doubt but that such a wife is one of the greatest assets to a man in the naval service."[2]

In a section defining the ideal naval household, the authors focused on the duties of the competent wife:

> Depending upon your hours of rising and the time of breakfast, after which you see your hero off to work, two hours should give you ample time to do your daily routine housework thoroughly. Of course, if you stop to finish a detective story or go back to bed for an extra nap, remember to deduct it from your leisure instead of skipping your household duties. . . .
>
> Dinner should be a restful meal, gracious and peaceful and not interrupted by frequent trips to the kitchen. A weary husband may enjoy a cocktail or highball before dinner, or it

---

[1] Anne Briscoe Pye and Nancy Shea, *The Navy Wife* (New York, New York: Harper & Brothers, 1955), p. 191.

[2] Ibid., p. xii.

may be equally restful for him to have a quiet talk with you as an unhurried companion. Sometimes he may like to listen to the radio, and make informal remarks on the news to you. Even if you don't agree with his views, save your comments until after dinner. A good meal improves a man's disposition. You can make this before-dinner interlude a period of charm and relaxation to which your husband will look forward if you plan intelligently. Have your domestic machinery so well-oiled that you can take it easy before dinner.[3]

For the most part, I believed the book and vowed to fulfill its ideals.

After Gene was commissioned, he was sent on brief billets to Kansas and California. Then our baby Donald was born. When Donald was a month old we were transferred to Great Lakes Training Center in North Chicago, Illinois.

It was December, and the complex of concrete Navy apartments to which we were assigned was as drab as the month. Our ground floor apartment had two bedrooms, one bath, a kitchen with an eating area, and a small living room. The black tile floor with white streaks flowed through the apartment like an inky lake with whitecaps. The day we moved in I had been without a drink for eight months.

On Sunday morning, a week after our arrival, we walked to Wilbur and Mollie Lowes' for brunch. They lived in the same complex and Wilbur worked with Gene. Wilbur met us at the door with a hearty handshake, brought us to the living room (which was a duplicate of ours, even down to the black tile) and called his wife. Mollie, a stubby woman, trotted out from the bedroom, smiling and panting and running her fingers over her thin hair, which clung to her head like a cloche. She and Wilbur led us to the living room couch, then Wilbur brought us tall glasses of tomato juice with lemon slices floating on the top. I knew at the first swallow that they were Bloody Marys.

I thought about my eight-month abstinence from liquor and the ensuing good relationship between Gene and me. *I should give this back to Wilbur and ask for straight juice,* I thought. But I didn't. Soon I felt relaxed and happy and

[3] Ibid., p. 139, 140.

sensed that the drink was a prelude to a great visit. *One drink won't hurt a thing,* I thought. *I've abstained for months and tomorrow I'll continue abstaining. This drink's just a brief hiatus, like a split second plucked from a day.*

In the hour before brunch, each time my glass was empty I held it out to Wilbur. By the time we sat down to Eggs Benedict, I was drunk and verbose. I complimented Mollie on her lovely food, shining windows, smart dress, and beautiful hair. A grim look entered Gene's eyes. *He probably doesn't like thin hair,* I thought.

I felt marvelous. I was planning to stay the entire afternoon, but immediately after Mollie refilled our coffee cups, Gene said, "We've got to go. I've got to go through some papers from work."

"Can't you do them tonight?" I asked.

"No, they can't wait."

I knew they could wait, for Friday, when Gene had brought them home, he had said that he had a couple of hours of paperwork. He would have plenty of time tonight. "They can, too," I said.

"These can't."

"That's not true," I said.

"Muriel!" he snapped, and I gave up.

The minute we got out on the Lowes' stoop, Gene confronted me. "You're drunk."

"I'm not."

"You were gushing all over Mollie."

"I was being kind." I felt misunderstood, like a saint mistaken for a bank robber.

"You were drunk."

"I was being friendly. You've got a rotten attitude. If you don't staighten out and get friendly, you'll lose every friend you've got."

Gene exhaled in a rush, then spun around, stepped off the stoop, and strode rapidly along the sidewalk. I hurried along behind him, never quite catching up.

Late in the afternoon after I had slept off the drinks, I went to Gene at the kitchen table, where he was working on his papers. I said, "I'm sorry. I didn't mean to get drunk."

"I thought you were abstaining."

"I am."

"I wish you would. I don't want to go back to the way it was."

"We won't."

"There's Donny to consider."

I started to cry. "I wouldn't do anything to hurt him. I love him."

At the sight of my tears he pulled me into his lap and said, "I know that, darling."

The next morning snow spilled from an iron sky and brushed against the window. I was on the living room couch, and Donny was lying in my arm, sucking his bottle. Standing, I balanced the bottle under my chin, leaned over, and switched on the radio to catch the weather report. I sighed. Four inches had fallen and four more were predicted. I walked to the window. Snow rimmed my bicycle and spread like a sheet across the courtyard; the forecast was probably correct.

I watched the flakes and remembered how I had gushed over Mollie's food and windows and thin hair. I winced. Even if Mollie and Wilbur were the kindest people in Illinois, they were bound to think I was a screwball. *I can't face them again,* I thought. Great Lakes was a large base; maybe I could skirt them the next few years.

Then I remembered the Bloody Marys, the relaxed feeling, the happiness—really an exhilaration, as if I were a bird dipping through sunlight. I looked at the drab sky. With a few drinks it would light up, and it and I would be more than we were.

So I decided I would have a few drinks now and then. Just a few so that I could be a good mother—and a good wife. A few would not upset Gene. I glanced at the swirling snow, wondering if I dared drive to the liquor store. *I shouldn't take Donny out,* I thought. But I had to, because we had no liquor—not even a can of beer.

We went and I bought a bottle of Jim Beam. I skidded only twice, and both times I slid into the curb and did not damage the car. At home I put the Jim Beam in the cabinet under the kitchen sink.

That night while Gene and I played cribbage in the kitchen, I watched the clock on the wall. Eight seemed a good hour for a nightcap or two. At eight, I laid down my cards, walked casually to the sink—as if I were going for a glass of water—

bent, and lifted the Jim Beam from the cabinet. "Like one?" I asked offhandedly.

"Where did you get that? I thought we were out."

"I found it when I unpacked. I forgot to say anything." The lie came so easily.

"You said yesterday was an accident. You said you're stopping."

"I am—mostly."

"What does 'mostly' mean?"

"I mean mostly I'm not drinking. I don't think a drink or two a day can hurt me."

"If you can keep it there."

"I will. Do you want one?"

"No thanks."

We finished the game and I fixed another drink. Until Gene went to bed, the two were all I had. But then I went at the bourbon in earnest. My reality took a lovely turn and I went from unpretty to pretty, from unintelligent to intelligent, from insecure to secure and I loved myself.

I became ethereal. My mind bubbled with creativity and I brought a pen and paper to the kitchen table. I would write a cookbook filled with exotic recipes, ones no earthling could cook, because the ingredients would be stored in the above and beyond plane where my thoughts were. Only certain people, ones like me, would understand the book. At one point I wrote, "Puree six elf's whiskers, three hairs from a thirteen-eyed fly and six ounces of pulp from a loopola, a fruit which tastes like a banana, but looks like a doughnut. Served on toast, this blend will please the finicky eaters in your family."

While I poured bourbon after bourbon, recipes tumbled from my mind onto paper until I blacked out. In the morning I awoke to a faint cry that rose in volume like an oncoming freight. I thought, *What? What?* Then I realized that it was Donny crying from his bassinet beside me. Pushing up onto my elbows, I blinked at the dresser lamp, which glowed with the strength of the sun, then sat full up. My stomach rolled. I had a terrible hangover. Donny was beating the air with his hands. His face was red and wrinkled like a walnut. Apparently, he was hungry.

While I lowered my legs over the side of the bed, Gene walked in carrying a bottle of milk. He wore white boxer shorts and a white shirt. A diaper was slung over his shoulder. "It's about time," he said.

I glanced at the clock—7:00. "About time for what?"

"For you to wake up."

"I always wake up at seven."

Gene bent, lifted Donny from the bassinet, and pushed the bottle into his mouth. "What was going on last night?"

I strained to remember, then recalled the bourbons, the recipes. "Nothing much that I know about," I said, not anxious to tell him the truth.

"Really?" he said, his face flushing as it did when he was angry. "Nothing much, you say. Nothing much, and while Donny screamed for his middle-of-the-night bottle, you lay six inches from his head like a dead woman."

"I was tired. I stayed up late."

"Look, don't lie. You were drunk. I don't have time for this." He handed me Donny's bottle. "I need to get ready for work."

I took Donny and said, "I'm sorry. I didn't mean to get that way."

"What if you'd been alone with Donny? What if there'd been a fire?"

My stomach took a tumble. "I won't do it again."

"I hope not," he said and took the trousers of his uniform from a hanger. He pulled them on in choppy, angry movements, then left the room.

Because Gene was upset, I stayed sober for two days. But on the third day, after dinner, I had a few bourbons. I was exhausted from housework and I needed the relaxation. *Anybody would,* I thought.

From then on I drank every night and Donny's middle-of-the-night cries sailed past me and woke Gene.

One morning Gene found a stack of my recipes in the kitchen. "You write these stupid things?" he asked.

"Sometimes."

"Incredible."

"I don't mean to write them. I'm trying to stop."

"Stop? That's a nonsensical statement."

"I mean I'm trying to stop drinking so I won't write them."

But I didn't try to stop drinking. I wasn't, as I had hoped, a loving, competent wife. The cycle of my drinks, our fights, my sorries and Gene's forgiveness was fully in effect. He began to put in longer hours at work, as if forgiving was taking something from his pride which had to be replaced by high job performance. Though I dimly understood, I was too hooked to stop drinking. And I assumed he loved me too much to leave me.

CHAPTER III

I balanced on my tiptoes, reaching for a shoe box on the highest shelf in the closet. In it were my black spiked heels. "Can you come here?" I asked Gene. "I can't get this box."

"Which box?"

"The one on top. The brown one with the white letters."

Gene lifted it down. We were dressing for Captain Davis's cocktail party. During the five months we had been at Great Lakes, we had attended three cocktail parties, all gala events with plenty of food and liquor. I expected that Captain Davis's party would be equally gala and lavish.

I put on my new dress, a black shantung with a fitted waist, a full skirt, and a wide bow that tied at the neck. This was the first time Gene had seen it and I twirled before him, flaring the skirt flat out like a saucer. "Like it?" I asked.

"I love it," Gene said, reaching for me.

But I jumped away from his hand, wavered on the spindly heels, and said, "Stop it. Our baby-sitter's going to be here in a second." I smiled, though, enjoying the play.

Gene came after me and kissed my neck. "You're beautiful, gal."

I put my arms around him. "Really, she's almost here."

"I could call and cancel."

I laughed. The doorbell rang and I rushed from the room. "Hurry up and finish dressing," I called from the hall. Then from farther on down the hall I shouted, "Have I ever met Captain Davis? I don't remember."

Gene shouted, "Once, I think. At the reception for new officers."

33

At Captain Davis's home a teenage girl answered our ring and led us to the edge of the large living room. Gene leaned close and said, "Take it easy on the drinks."

"Of course!" I snapped.

"Don't get huffy."

"Then don't—" I started to say but was interrupted by Captain Davis.

"Hello there. Glad you could come, Gene, and hmmm, let's see—I've got it—Muriel," the captain boomed out. He was about five feet four and I wondered if, unconsciously, he boomed to compensate for his lack of height.

"Well, yes, now," he continued, "how's the little mother? It's the best time of your life. The very best. No other to match it." He patted Gene's shoulder and stretched his thin mouth into a long smile.

"We—" I said.

"Yes, of course, you want a drink. This way, Gene." Like a dingy pulling a sailboat, the captain bustled off with Gene in tow.

I started through the living room toward a group gathered next to a floor lamp. The living room was about thirty feet long and contained only the floor lamp, three table lamps, and three mahogany end tables. At this naval base it was common practice to remove the living room furniture before a large cocktail party. About forty people were grouped around the room, and the door bell continued to ring.

I kept well to the left side of the room, as Wilbur and Mollie Lowe were to the right, in front of the fireplace. Whenever I saw them, I felt foolish. But despite my best efforts to avoid them, we had met at a couple of gatherings.

Gene touched my shoulder and handed me a pale bourbon and water, mostly water. "What kind of drink is that?" I said, keeping my voice low.

"A *normal* drink."

"It is not!" I snapped. But my irritation left quickly, for at least it was a drink.

We both stepped up to a group. There was Tom Page, a hulking young man, and Ruth Coogan, also young and evidently in love with Tom. Standing slightly behind them was Janet Hack, a kind-looking woman in her early forties. Janet acknowledged Gene and me with a nod and turned back to Tom and Ruth.

"I run three miles before work," Tom was saying.

"That's wonderful," said Ruth, her eyes fixed on Tom.

"I never miss a day," he added.

"Neither do I," said Ruth.

"Nor I," said Janet.

I didn't comment, because I neither ran nor exercised. I felt inferior.

I stepped away and went to the kitchen to fix a drink. I poured a few ounces of bourbon in a glass and topped it with Coke to hide the quantity of bourbon. I drank half of it, then poured in more bourbon, more Coke and started back to Tom, Ruth, and Janet. I met Gene on the way. Studying my glass, he said, "Coke?"

"Not exactly," I said, irritated. This was his second comment about my drinks. What was wrong with him? Why didn't he relax and let me have a little fun? Then for a moment, I understood. Earlier, he had wanted to stay home. But then I thought, *No, it isn't that.* He was nagging me because he was nervous and overpressured by his navy work, his evening classes at Northwestern, his homework. (Gene was now working toward a master's in business administration.)

"Calm down and leave me alone," I said and rejoined Ruth, Tom, and Janet, who were now discussing running shoes. After several swallows of the drink, I felt up to their running ability and said, "I used to trot ten times around my high school track." That was a lie, but I felt good about it. The truth was that every month or so I had run four laps and collapsed on the grass.

Ruth and Tom nodded, as though impressed and Janet Hack said, "That was a good run."

"It was," I said.

A couple of drinks later, feeling wonderful about myself, I began to circulate. To a group standing in front of the French doors, I said, "When Gene and I were first married, I headed a chemical lab in North Chicago."

"Quite a responsibility," said a tall woman with broad shoulders.

"Yes," I responded. "I hated to quit, but Gene got called into the Navy."

To a group near the dining room table, I said, "Someday I hope to become a fine writer, maybe even better than Melville, but not as good as Shakespeare. He's pretty good."

Two of the women smiled politely and a man with a round face said, "A peach of an ambition."

I continued to circulate, carefully staying away from Gene. But well into the evening, I saw his belt, then his shoes, as I bent down, spread my fingers flat against the carpet, straightened my legs, and pulled my knees together. In an effort to further impress Janet Hack, I was demonstrating my toe-touching technique. Gene lifted me up by the elbow. "We'll be right back," he told Janet.

Grasping my arm he steered me to an empty corner. "How many have you had?"

"Just a few."

"You're lying. Why are you touching your toes? This isn't a gym."

I stared at him and my head spun. I said, "Toes can be touched anywhere."

"We're leaving. Where's your purse?"

"We're not," I said.

"We *are* going." His tone was hard, obstinate. Though it seemed senseless to me, I concurred.

I found Captain Davis and said, "Gene's looking for my purse, because we've got to go—he's tired from all his homework at school. We had the best time we've ever had. We'd like you to come and visit us sometime." I paused and glanced at Gene, who had returned with my purse. His eyes were wide with either embarrassment or wonder. After deciding that it was wonder brought on by my gracious good-bye, I continued, "The ham and turkey and those hors d'oeuvres—"

"I appreciate your thanks," Captain Davis said, "but I'm not your host."

Confused, I said, "You're not?"

"It'll be Captain Davis you want to thank."

"You look like Captain Davis," I said. I was dizzy and drunk. "I guess maybe Captain Davis is shorter," I said.

"My wife's a little mixed-up," Gene said.

"An easy mistake to make," the man replied.

"Well, excuse us," Gene said.

"Of course."

The man walked away and I said, "Who is he?"

"Captain Jensen."

"It was an easy mistake to make."

In anger he barked, "It was not. Captain Jensen's six inches taller and fifty pounds heavier than Captain Davis."

"If you were in a room full of my friends, you'd thank the wrong person too."

Without answering, Gene grabbed my arm and sped me through the door and to the car.

I said, "We should go back and thank Captain Davis."

"I'll thank him Monday."

"It was an easy mistake."

"Enough, Muriel. It's not that you thanked the wrong man. It's that you're plastered."

"I am not."

"Cut it."

"I want to discuss it."

We drove home in silence.

In the morning under a warm sun and a sky as blue as a swimming pool, Gene had Donny out crawling in the grass. I was drooped on the couch, watching them and thinking. If only I hadn't gotten drunk and raced around lying and misthanking. *Captain Jensen must think I'm a fool. I was one,* I thought. I could never face him again.

If only Gene weren't so upset. After getting up, he had gone to the kitchen, rattled around, then yelled, "Where's the coffeepot?"

Then before taking Donny out, Gene had asked, "Where's my toolbox?"

That was about all he had said to me.

I felt as if Gene and I were on the Sahara, with the air shimmering in heat waves and the sand ridged by the wind. As if Gene were a mile away, screaming, "Where's my toolbox?" Unless I brought him the box, we would remain separated.

In August, three months after Captain Davis's cocktail party and an hour or so after Gene went to bed, I lay on the couch drinking a can of beer. It was muggy, the air so still that the curtains were flat against the window. I picked up a magazine and fanned myself.

When I cooled down a little, I went to the window and

looked at the apartment on the other side of the courtyard. Here and there a light shone, but most people were in bed. None of them knew I watched and I felt partly as if I spied, partly as if I were omniscient, like God.

That is, if there is a God, I thought. *From the beginning of time on, man has created gods. Chances are, God just exists in a person's mind.*

But I hated to believe that. I wanted God to exist, to listen to man, to me. If that were so, right then I could say, "I'd like to talk to You."

And God would say, "I'm listening, Muriel."

And I would tell Him my worry. "I think I might be drinking too much sometimes. I think I might need Your help."

"I'll help you," God would say.

With a feeling of caring for God catching at my throat, I went to the coffee table, set my beer can down, and knelt. I bent my head and prayed, "God, please help me. Please speak to me."

I scanned the corners of the room and glanced at the motionless curtains, looking for God. But I didn't see Him. I closed my eyes and concentrated on hearing His voice, but He didn't speak. I waited. I gave Him time. Finally I opened my eyes and tears ran down my cheeks.

Anger followed regret, and I thought, *If God does exist, He's silent, invisible, and as impersonal as a tree. I'll never pray again.*

I went to the kitchen and opened a can of beer. I was still crying.

That same August, I became pregnant, and the following May I gave birth to a girl, Deborah Lynne. Though I loved her and Donny, I found it difficult to give them my full attention because every morning I had a hangover.

Having a hangover was like having the flu. I had one now. It was 8:00 a.m. and Donny was calling, "Mommy, Mommy," and Debbie was crying and I was pushing myself out of bed. My head ached and my mouth felt as if I had been sucking on a ball of cotton. I went to the kitchen, poured a glass of soda, then went to the bedroom and let down the side of Donny's crib. While I dressed and fed the children, my stomach rolled and my muscles ached. I had gone to bed at 3:00 a.m. and I was exhausted. I had to get more sleep.

I lifted Debbie from the living room couch, took Donny's hand, and brought them to their bedroom. I locked the door, laid Debbie in her bassinet, scattered Donny's toys on the floor, and climbed into his crib. In order to fit, I turned on my side and drew up my legs. It was a snug fit, but it would do. I slept.

But not for long. Donny began poking at my face, "Get up, Mommy. Get up."

"Soon," I mumbled. "Let's see your truck catch your doggie."

Diverted, he played awhile and I slept—until he poked me again. "Up, Mommy. Get up."

"Okay, in a minute. Can you make a train with your blocks?"

I shut my eyes again.

About an hour and a half after we came in, Donny began to whine, evidently hating that he was confined and ignored. He tugged at my arm. "Up, Mommy. Up, Mommy. Up, Mommy—"

"Okay, okay." I climbed out, not feeling perfect, but well enough to face the day.

The morning sleep in the crib became a routine. During that time the phone often rang, but I didn't answer it. One afternoon Gene phoned and said, "It's almost impossible to reach you in the morning. Where are you?"

"I'm busy with the kids."

"Too busy to answer the phone?"

"Yes. Please don't ever call before noon."

CHAPTER IV

On a windy afternoon when Donny was 28 months old, I was sitting cross-legged on the living room carpet. Beyond the window, scraps of paper skittered over the grass in the courtyard, and the young maples beside the sidewalk swayed like dancers. I was shaking the contents of my purse onto a newspaper. Out fluttered the usual paraphernalia and some change—two dimes, two nickels, three pennies. I threw everything back into my purse, including the change, and hurried to our bedroom, pulled open Gene's top dresser drawer, and shuffled through a clutter of belts and papers. In the corner under a telephone message from his office were six cents. I picked them up. I now had just thirty-nine cents and no liquor. I had to find more money.

I searched through coat and pants pockets, drawers—even lay on the floor and looked under the bed. No money.

As I started toward the kitchen to take another look in the silverware drawer, I remembered the two silver dollars packed in a white box in the bottom drawer of Gene's desk. And I remembered the day Gene had put them there. "I got them from the bank," he had said.

"What for?" I asked.

"For the kids. They commemorate their birth years. They're for their eighteenth birthdays."

"I like that."

Gene had grinned with pleasure. "It'll be something special from their dad."

How could I spend the silver dollars? But the silverware drawer was empty, and I found myself hurrying into the bedroom and to Gene's desk. I pulled open the drawer and lifted out the box. *Just looking,* I thought, as I took off the lid, removed the dollars, and laid them in my palm. As if by reflex, I closed my hand around them and kicked the drawer shut.

I dropped the dollars in my purse. What else could I do? I would replace them and Gene would never know the difference. One silver dollar looked just like another silver dollar.

Donny and Debbie and I drove in our Volkswagen to the liquor store. Donny's eyes lighted with excitement as we walked into Creekway Liquor Market, a long, narrow store with three rows of bottle-filled shelves. He loved the bottles, especially the bright liqueurs and wines. "I want some booze," he said, reaching for a bottle of shimmery green creme de menthe.

"Don't touch the bottles. They're no-no's." I pulled his hand from the creme de menthe. "And don't say 'booze,' " I whispered, feeling shame; "booze" was an unnatural word for a two-year-old, the kind of word the child of a drinking mother might overhear and repeat.

"I want that booze!" he yelled.

"Shh, shh," I said and at the same time noticed an elderly man watching us from the end of the aisle. He looked like Papa Hansen, my grandfather.

I smiled at the man. "He thinks booze is pop."

"Ohh," said the man.

"I want that booze! I want that booze! I want that booze!" Donny screeched.

"Shh, shh," I said, and then to the man, "He drinks quite a bit of pop."

"Booze, booze, booze!"

The man drew the lines on his forehead into crossroads of disapproval. *He thinks I'm an unfit mother,* I thought. *If only he could see my clean apartment, the wholesome meals I fix, the five motherless puppies that I've nursed to health—and my husband, an ensign in the United States Navy.*

I turned to Donny and snapped, "Quiet down!"

Donny sank to the floor, threw himself on his back, and pounded the floor with his heels. I stepped over him and rushed to the rear of the store, where I picked up two six-packs of beer. After paying for the beer with the silver dollars, I left with Debbie in one arm, the beer in the other, and Donny trailing behind, whimpering. I felt like a bag of rotten pears.

When Gene came home from work, he found me in the kitchen washing lettuce. He stood behind me, kissed the back of my neck, and wrapped his arms around me. "How was your day?" he said.

"Terrible. I'm exhausted."

"What happened?"

"Donny acted like a brat. He had a tantrum at the store and everyone stared at him. I felt like an idiot."

"What store were you at?"

"The commissary." The lie, as did many lies these days, came out easily.

In sympathy Gene turned me around and kissed me. He said he would keep Donny out of the kitchen while I fixed dinner.

Much later, I was lying on the couch, drinking the last can of beer from the six-packs and feeling as light as whipped cream. *A good gust of air,* I thought, *could lift me off the couch and on up to the ceiling. But with my luck*—I laughed—*I'd bounce against the plaster and wake Gene. And he'd run out and pull me from the ceiling and yell, "Find another way to entertain yourself!"* Which reminded me . . .

There was an unfinished discussion between Gene and me. Last night I had told him that I planned to become an advertising executive. He had said I was nuts. But tonight I would catch his attention and spark his enthusiasm. I would explain that, even though I did not have a college degree or writing experience, I had the brains and talent to climb sky-high in advertising.

I'll tell him, I thought, as I stood up, padded across the carpet, onto the black tile, and along the hallway, aiming my feet carefully so that I wouldn't topple into a wall. *I'll catch his attention,* I thought as I swayed into the bedroom. I flipped on the light switch, swung toward the bed, and climbed in.

Gene was sleeping on his back, and giving stentorious snores. I crawled across the bed, straddled his stomach, and shook his shoulders. "Ahh, ahh," he moaned as his head bounced up and down. Sometimes it was difficult to wake Gene. Finally he opened his eyes. "What is it?" he mumbled.

I bent down until my eyes were inches from his and barked out, "My plan to be an advertising executive is not nuts. I'm smart and I can do it. Your sour attitude's not going to stop me. Someday I'll have a large office and three secretaries."

"Get off my stomach and go away," Gene muttered.

"I won't leave until I'm finished. You'll listen until you tell me I can make it."

"Go away!" he shouted.

"No." I grabbed his shoulders and tightened my legs against his sides. "You'll never get rid of me."

"Leave!" With a great thrust, Gene rolled to his side, throwing me onto the mattress. He pulled his pillow from under his head and clamped it on top of his head.

"All right," I said, sliding off the bed. I lifted my head high and said with dignity, "I was about to go anyhow."

I went back to the couch, finished the can of beer, and stretched out on my back. *Gene is obnoxious,* I thought. *He deserves losing the silver dollars.* If he ever asked where they had gone, I would say, "There's been a terrible robbery. I'm missing a few things myself."

I got a pencil and listed the items taken in the robbery: 2 silver dollars, 2 cashmere sweaters, 1 silver pitcher, 9 books . . .

The impact of the robbery hit and I cried. I crumpled the list and threw it on the floor. I didn't understand myself. In order to drink, I lied, stole—what next? Was I becoming an alcoholic, like Dad and Mom and Aunt Red?

I remembered an Alcoholics Anonymous meeting in my parents' living room. It had been my father's group; Mom had not attended A.A. meetings. The talk and laughter had come to Chris, Ellen, and me in the kitchen; Ellen, who was four, nine years my junior, had asked, "Will Daddy stay sober?"

"I think so," I said.

"He will," said Chris. "I know he will."

After attending A.A. for five months, Dad started drinking again. And one morning while he was at the kitchen table, his shoulders bent with the round-the-clock drinking of the previous two weeks, I asked, "Why don't you go back to the meetings?"

He lifted his head and smiled, for he was a gentle drunk. "In the Depression for 25 cents, Henry and I could buy—"

"The meetings, Dad. You should go back."

"Fix me a little one, Mewy, just a short one."

"Please give them another chance."

"Just a short one." He measured an inch with his finger and thumb, and I gave up and filled his glass about an inch.

My thoughts came back to the present. With a rush of honesty, I knew that I was as committed to alcohol as Dad. But I did not want to be like him. I stood and dropped my beer can on the carpet and crushed it. That can was my last. I would quit drinking. Tomorrow I would call Alcoholics Anonymous.

In the morning I had second thoughts: I was only twenty-four, years too young to be an alcoholic. And even if I were an alcoholic, I couldn't call a stranger for help. But I forced myself to pick up the phone directory and find Alcoholics Anonymous. My heart pounded and my hands perspired when I saw the number. I dialed. Clay, a man with a voice that scratched like a worn record, answered the phone. He invited me to a meeting that evening and said that a woman from the group would be phoning me. I hung up, drained.

It was Mary who phoned. She breathlessly offered to pick me up at 7:45, then said, "I'm sorry I can't talk longer, but I've got an appointment with my son's English teacher."

That evening, shortly before Mary was due, I was sitting on the couch nervously swinging my foot back and forth. Because I wanted to go into A.A. with a clean conscience, I was telling Gene about the silver dollars. "I didn't mean to take them," I said, "but I needed the money for some beer. I didn't really know what I was doing until after I did it. I'll go to the bank and get two more. I'm really sorry. I want to go to A.A. and get a new start."

Gene pulled me up from the couch and into his arms. "You've got my full support, gal."

"Then you don't mind about the dollars?"

"I mind, but the important thing is that you're going to A.A."

I laid my head in the hollow of his shoulder and felt the strength of his love for me. I almost loved him.

"I'm proud of you," he said. "It's a big step."

All at once I felt the immensity of the step and I craved a drink. *I'm only twenty-four and I'm not old enough to be an alcoholic,* I thought. "Don't be too proud," I said. "I'm just trying this out. I don't know what the meeting will be like."

"Of course, darling." He lifted my chin and kissed me, obviously not noting my trepidation.

"Mary should be here now," I said. I smoothed down my hair and went to the closet for my coat. As I took it from a hanger the door bell rang. "See you later," I called and pulled open the door.

In my mind, Mary had been a floozy in a bright pink dress with a limp cigarette dangling from the corner of her mouth. Not that I expected that a woman who rushed off to see her son's English teacher was a floozy, but still, Mary came out that way in my mind. But here was a plain woman in her late forties, wearing a drab raincoat and sensible pumps.

"Muriel?" she asked. I nodded. "It's good to meet you. We're running late." I trailed her quick-stepping pumps to her car.

As we pulled away from the curb, she explained that we were heading for a church near downtown North Chicago. "I've been going to meetings there for seven years," she said.

"Oh," I said, feeling nervous and tongue-tied.

Mary sensed my feelings. "Apprehensive?"

"Yes. I keep thinking I might not be old enough to be an alcoholic. I'm only twenty-four."

"It's not a matter of age. It's a matter of reaching one's bottom."

"You mean the end of your rope?"

"Exactly. I didn't reach mine until I was committed to Elgin [an insane asylum]."

Though Mary had an over-hurried manner, thus was probably high-strung, she was so ordinary in looks and speech that it was impossible to imagine her in an asylum. Shocked, I blurted out, "Why, what happened?"

"I had D.T.'s.* The doctor said I had to quit drinking or I'd lose my mind—I would become a walking vegetable." She glanced at me, her eyes solemn. "You don't have to go my route. You can be smarter."

In Mary's high-strung manner, I saw myself. *I could be heading her way,* I thought, and I determined to quit drinking.

Soon Mary swung her car around a corner and pulled up to a curb beside a white brick church. "We're here," she said,

---

Delirium tremens: a violent, delirious state caused by excessive intake of alcohol.

and I followed her inside, down a flight of stairs, and into a large room.

To the left side of the room, next to a concrete-block wall, about twenty-five men and women were seated at three tables pushed end to end. Most drank coffee from thick, white mugs. Most smoked, and the smoke fogged the air. I was the youngest person there.

I stopped at the coffeepot with Mary for a mug of coffee, then took a seat between her and a barrel-chested man. He touched my arm and said, "New? I haven't seen you here before."

"This is my first meeting," I whispered, for the chairman, a man of about fifty, had just rapped a gavel against the table and was now standing.

We all rose and recited "The Serenity Prayer": " 'God grant me the serenity to accept the things I cannot change; courage to change the things I can, and wisdom to know the difference.' "*

Except for the chairman, we all sat. "I'm Clay and I'm an alcoholic," he said. *So he's Clay,* I thought and once again noted his scratchy voice. Clay lighted a cigarette, welcomed us to the High Street Group, and explained that the sole purpose of A.A. was to help its members achieve sobriety. The only requirement for membership was a desire to stop drinking. "Most of us stay sober with the help of a Higher Power," he said. He paused and then asked, "Does anyone have something he'd like to bring up for discussion?"

The barrel-chested man said, "There's a new person here. I think we should talk about the importance of staying away from the first drink."

Please don't point me out—please don't do anything special for me, I thought.

To my relief I wasn't identified. No one objected to the topic and Clay began the discussion. "A few months after I came to A.A., I decided I could handle a drink. I couldn't. I ended up on a four-week binge." After Clay told us about the binge, he called on the man to his right, the man next to him, and so

---

*Adapted by the A.A.'s from Reinhold Niebuhr's poem, "Prayer for Serenity."

on. When I realized his method, I counted. He would get to me five turns from now. The prospect of speaking terrified me. My hands perspired. What should I say?

Should I tell them about my first drink at Mr. and Mrs. Staceys' when I was fourteen? While baby-sitting their two boys, I found the liquor cabinet in the dining room. Thinking it would be daring to have a drink, I poured a bourbon and ginger ale. It was delicious. From then on, each time I baby-sat, I took out a bottle of liquor, poured a few ounces into a glass, and replaced the missing liquor with water. To keep Mr. and Mrs. Staceys' bottles from becoming over-diluted, I drank from a different bottle each time. The Staceys never questioned me.

Or should I tell the group about the alcoholics in my family: Dad, Mom, Aunt Red, my uncle, my grandmother, and seven second cousins.

Soon it was my turn. Clay gave me a kind look and said, "Are you the young lady who phoned this morning?" I nodded. "I'm glad you came. Would you like to make a comment?"

"Yes—I would." I blushed, my voice trembled and the cigarette I held shook so violently that I dropped it in an ashtray. I knew that everyone was watching me falter. I managed to add, "I'm glad to be here," then fixed my eyes on the table-top.

Worried because I had trembled in front of twenty-five people, I didn't hear the comments that followed. What would they be thinking of me? I pulled a cigarette from my pack and dragged on it until it was a butt. I lighted another, smoked, watched the smoke spiral to the ceiling. In my self-concern, I heard nothing until a woman with white, upswept hair and perfect makeup spoke. She was the last person to comment. Her elegance captured my attention. "I've been sober now for three years," she said. "One drink would lead to my death. When I came to A.A., my liver was beginning to go. It was cirrhosis. I looked as if I were pregnant. For me it was a choice of sobriety or death. I chose to live."

She chose to live, I thought, touched, yet at the same time relieved that I was not pressed into making the choice. For I wasn't tottering on the brink of cirrhosis, and my stomach was as flat as the tabletop. Right then I knew I was too healthy and young for A.A.

Thank heavens, I thought as the group stood and recited the Lord's Prayer. The prayer ended the meeting.

Before Mary and I left, she suggested I buy a copy of *Alcoholics Anonymous.* "It's the A.A. bible," she said. To please Mary, I bought one. When she had parked beside the curb in front of my apartment, she wrote out her phone number and said, "Call me anytime. I'll give you a call in the morning."

In the apartment I sank onto the couch and Gene handed me a cup of coffee. "Every single muscle in my body aches," I said.

"From what?"

"From being nervous at the meeting, I guess."

"But you did like it?"

If I declared that I was quitting A.A., we would argue. I was too emotionally spent for that. Temporizing, I said, "It was okay. It's hard to know the first time just what it's like."

"Were there many women?"

"About five."

"Were there—?"

"I'm too tired to talk anymore about it tonight. I think I'll go to bed."

"I'll be in later."

"Homework?"

"I've got a finance exam coming up."

I remembered that I had no money to buy beer the next day. "May I have a few dollars for eggs and milk?"

Gene handed me ten dollars, kissed me, and said, "Good night, darling. I'm proud of you."

With his pride dragging at my heels, I walked to bed.

The next day at noon, Mary phoned. By that time there were two six-packs of beer in the refrigerator and a fifth of bourbon in the cabinet under the sink. "How are you feeling?" she said.

"Fine."

"Your body's withdrawing from alcohol and you might get a little jittery. You might crave a drink."

"I feel fine."

"Well, if it happens, have something sweet—honey or orange juice."

"I will."

"Pamper yourself. You're going through a hard time. And read *Alcoholics Anonymous.*"

"Yes, I will." I paused. "Mary?"

"Yes."

"I don't know how to say this, but I'm not going back to the meetings. I'm not old enough to be an alcoholic. I don't drink as much as the people in A.A. I can control myself."

"It's not a question of age or amount, but of tolerance. Can we tolerate the kind of morals and values that go along with drinking? Can we stand ourselves?"

"I've got no problems with my conscience." I was so set on drinking the beer in the refrigerator and the bourbon under the sink that I excused my lies, my theft.

Mary urged me to reconsider, but I wouldn't. She invited me to call if I changed my mind.

After Mary hung up, I lifted *Alcoholics Anonymous* from the coffee table. I was curious as to its contents, yet afraid that it would make me feel guilty about my plan to drink. I leafed through quickly. One page caught my eye and I read:

> We are convinced, to a man, that alcoholics of our type are in the grip of a progressive illness. Over any considerable period we get worse, never better. . . .
>
> Despite all we can say, many who are real alcoholics are not going to believe they are in that class. By every form of self-deception and experimentation, they will try to prove themselves exceptions to the rule, therefore nonalcoholic.[4]

I slammed the book shut, stalked into my bedroom. I pushed it under the bed, next to the wall where my dust mop would seldom touch it.

That evening while Gene, Donny and I raced trucks across the living room carpet, I decided the best way to approach my break with A.A. was to simply start drinking, as if that were normal. And it was. How else could I get rid of the jitters I'd had for a couple of days? I walked to the refrigerator and took out a beer. I brought it to the couch. Gene glanced up, opened his mouth in surprise, then said, "A beer?"

---

[4] Alcoholics Anonymous World Services, Inc., *Alcoholics Anonymous* (Cornwall, N.Y.: The Cornwall Press, Inc., 1955), pp. 30-31. Reprinted with permission of Alcoholics Anonymous World Services, Inc.

"Yes, a beer," I said. "I learned in A.A. that I can handle it if I watch myself."

Gene's voice snapped with annoyance. "Your sobriety's got the all-time record for shortness—less than two days."

I lifted the can and took a long, rebellious swallow. "What are you, a calendar?"

"And what exactly are you?"

His accusing remark infuriated me. "For one thing, I'm not an alcoholic. Those people drink far more than I'm ever going to. Your problem is you expect me to be a saint."

"Look, you went to that meeting because you wanted to. Nobody forced you. I was just hoping—"

Hot as fire, I shouted, "Hope about yourself and keep your hope off me!" I hated Gene and his hope.

"You're irrational!" he yelled.

"I can't stand you."

"I can't stand your drinking."

"Then get another wife—a Baptist. She'll sign a non-drinking pledge for you."

Donny's eyes widened in fright. "Mommy, Daddy, don't yell."

I picked up Donny, hugged him, and said to Gene, "Look what you've done."

"You're crazy." Gene jumped up, snatched his finance text from the coffee table, and stormed down the hall to the bedroom, slamming the door after him.

CHAPTER V

At 10:00 p.m. the next evening I was lying on the couch, drinking beer, waiting for Gene to return from his class at Northwestern. We had not spoken since the fight. But now I wanted to apologize so that I could drink in peace.

About 10:30 I heard the front door open. Springing up, I stuffed my can of beer under a pile of pillows next to the couch arm. "How was the finance exam?" I called cheerfully.

"A bit rough." I heard the closet door bang shut and Gene's shoes tap against the floor tile. Something heavy thumped onto the kitchen counter. The refrigerator door swished open. Bottles clanked.

"Are you hungry?" I called.

"No, I ate on the way to class. I'm getting a beer."

A beer? I thought. Given our stormy fight, why would he be getting a beer? Besides, when he was home, he was usually a teetotaler. I took my can from under the pillows. With him drinking there was no reason to hide it.

Gene came in, sat next to the pillows, and kicked off his shoes.

"Well . . . " I said and smiled.

"I'm giving in to it," he said. "If you can't fight it, join it. From now on I'll match you can for can, glass for glass. I bought a case of quarts on the way home."

"Don't talk like that," I said with mixed feelings—a feeling of gratitude, because there was a case of quarts in the house; a feeling of hysteria, because, if Gene drank like me, how would he get to work in the morning? How would we buy groceries? Pay rent?

"Glass for glass and can for can." With a flinty look in his eyes, Gene lifted his can and drained it in three long swallows. He jumped up, strode to the kitchen, got another can and returned. This time he finished the can in ten swallows. Again he hopped up and headed for the kitchen.

"Wait," I said. "I don't want you to be like me. Just because—" I started to cry.

"Because what?"

"Just because I left A.A., you don't have to act like you're acting."

"Go back to A.A., Muriel."

"I can't. I would, but I'm not an alcoholic. It's not the right place for me." He started through the doorway and I ran after him and caught him at the refrigerator. "Please—I promise I'll be careful. I'll limit myself."

I put my arms around his waist. I could feel the knobs of his spine set in a rigid line. Then all at once, he breathed out hard and I felt his spine bend. "It's your life," he said. "I can't carry you to the meetings."

"I won't need them. I'll be fine."

He drew back and I touched his cheek. "You still love me, don't you?" I begged. I couldn't love him, and I didn't love myself. But if Gene didn't love me, then what would I do?

"Yes," he said.

"If you did, you'd kiss me."

He kissed me on the cheek.

Gathering up my courage, I said, "Do you mind if I get another beer?"

"Muriel—for God's sake."

"But I thought that's what we were getting at. I said I'd be careful. This is only my second."

"Don't lie."

"I'm sorry. I guess it's my fourth or fifth."

"Then make this the last."

I saw that the fight was behind us and that if I had another beer, he would accept it.

While Gene put water on to boil for coffee, I got the beer.

"How was your finance exam?" I asked.

"It was a bear. We had just two hours to analyze a complex problem in the finances of each of three companies."

I knew Gene would get a B. He always got B's, and if he

had more time he'd probably get A's. As it was, he weekly squeezed in time to work forty hours at the base, drive the fifty miles to Northwestern three times, spend six hours in class, and study fifteen or more hours. But he was self-disciplined and self-controlled, emotionally capable of handling that load and more. He hoped someday to be a success in a corporation, not so much for the money as for the feeling of accomplishment.

Gene poured the boiling water into the coffeepot and I asked, "When do you get the test back?"

"Probably next week."

After the coffee had dripped through, we went to the living room couch. I tucked my legs under me and said, "Just think, you'll be out of the Navy in two months." I was quiet a minute, then said, "Are you going to take Dad's offer?" Dad's roofing business was doing well, and he had offered Gene a partnership.

"I told you a few days ago, I don't want to work with your dad."

"I thought maybe you'd change your mind. It's a good opportunity. Dad's got a lot of jobs coming in."

"I couldn't tolerate working with a person who goes off on six-week binges. I've got enough—"

"You're right," I said, knowing he would say that he had enough problems with my drinking. "It wouldn't work out."

"I'm going to send out résumés in a couple of days."

"To whom?"

"I don't know yet."

In the next two weeks Gene researched corporations, sent out résumés, and was invited to interview Procter & Gamble. He, of course, accepted the invitation, and late one afternoon, after an all-day interview, he strode in with a smile.

"They've offered you a job," I said, hurrying after him into the living room.

"They have," he said and tossed his suit coat over the arm of the couch. He loosened his tie, rolled up the sleeves of his white shirt, and sat with his arms stretched along the back of the couch.

"Great. As what?"

"As a planning engineer, to plan the materials and crews

necessary for maintenance and construction at the plant in Chicago."

"Did you take it?"

"Yes."

"Should you have?"

"You mean because I didn't interview anyone else?"

"Yes."

"I don't need to. I like P & G. They're what I'm looking for. They're large. They manufacture a wide range of products. They only promote from within the organization; they never hire a man at a promoted level. They—"

"What's the salary?"

He moved his arms to his sides and turned toward me. "Higher than you'll think."

In excited anticipation I said quickly, "What—what is it?"

"Six hundred and twenty-five a month."

"That much. That's great. That's—"

"That's seventy-five hundred a year."

I moved in under his arm. Against his white shirt his eyes seemed bluer, his face ruddier than usual. I saw his confidence, and I felt pride in being his wife. "We'll celebrate," I said. "I'll cook a fancy dinner."

I broiled lobster tails, tossed a green salad with butter-fried croutons and sieved eggs, and baked blueberry muffins. We ate by candlelight and drank champagne and planned Gene's rise to plant manager or higher. I felt love for him. He, in becoming important, would bring importance to me. And I would then like myself.

We left the Navy in May and moved into a small apartment, then to a larger apartment where our third child, Douglas, was born. When Douglas was three months old, we bought a three-bedroom ranch in Elmhurst on Spring Road, about a mile from my parents' home. Our house had a screened porch, and a narrow living room with a fieldstone fireplace and worn brown carpeting. The garage was detached from the house, as were most of the garages on Spring Road. And the basement was sectioned into a work area, a bathroom, and a family room with pine walls and a bar—which I stocked with liquor, glasses and mixes.

Our house was 22 miles from Procter & Gamble's Chicago

plant. For Gene, via the Congress Expressway, it was a 40-minute drive in the morning and a 60- to 90-minute drive in the evening. The commute, 50-hour work week, classes at Northwestern, and studying kept Gene constantly busy, which was fine with me. I wanted as little attention as possible on my drinking.

Two years passed with Gene occasionally blowing up as he noted a mark in my downward slide. But he was too busy to take in the full depth and thus take any action—like leaving.

Then in my twenty-ninth year on a Saturday night in October, Gene and I were driving home from an evening of bridge with our friends, the Hoods. I was drunk and Gene was sober. It was close to 2:00 a.m., and the normally busy streets were almost deserted. The black sky threatened stormy weather.

I stared at the sky and thought about Chris, my sister who now had four boys and one girl. Almost everyone said, "Chris does a wonderful job with her children. Chris is such a lovely person." *If I had two or three more babies,* I thought, *then people would say I was a wonderful, lovely person.*

Keeping my gaze on the sky, I said to Gene, "Douglas is two and Donny's almost seven, and Debbie's five. They're getting old."

"So?"

"I want another baby."

"What!" he sputtered. "We've got enough."

"We can afford them."

"It's not money, it's ability. You're barely able to manage three."

Becoming angry, I turned my eyes on Gene, and commanded, "We will have another child—probably *two* more children."

"We will not. You're hung over every morning and drunk every night. There's no possible way you could take care of a baby. Look at you now. You're half-lit."

"I am not."

"Then why did you ask the Hoods to come see your shoes? Does a sober person ask that? Does she?"

"She could—just because you're not a shoe connoisseur—"

"Ridiculous."

"It's not ridiculous, it's normal." Then leaning toward

Gene so that he would catch my point, I said, "Chris's got five kids. We've got only three."

"So, you're in competition with your sister. That's unbelievable."

For a few moments I thought about the word "unbelievable." All of a sudden an uncontainable surge of melody came and I sang, "Too unbelievable for anybody."

"Stop that." Gene's face was as stormy as the sky.

I tried to stop, but I couldn't. "Too unbelievable for you—"

"Cut it right now. You sound like a maniac." Magically my ears had grown filters which diluted his anger into mild displeasure.

"I sing because I'm joyful. I sing—"

"Cut it out!" Gene yelled. He must have yelled because I heard his voice squeak. He steered the car sharply to the right and pulled off the road. While he turned the key in the ignition, I decided to quit speaking entirely. From now on I would only sing. In fact, I would write a whodunit in which the dialogue was completely in lyrics, *The Singing Detective.*

As I thought about the book, I remembered Aunt Red sitting on the floor singing, "I'm better than an orange, better than a carrot." Was I becoming like Aunt Red? My spirits sagged, but I pulled them up fast with a no. In no way, shape, or form was I like Aunt Red.

"Muriel," Gene said, "if you continue with this drinking . . ." He paused, then continued in a hard voice, "It's getting to the point where you're pushing me too far."

"I only asked for a baby."

"This is impossible. You're senseless."

"Don't be crabby."

Gene started up the car and shoved the gearshift into first. He drove home in silence while I sang lyrics for the book.

At home, he zipped from the car and on into bed without speaking.

In the morning, rain drilled against the window, waking me but not Gene. The air seemed damp and cold, as if a fog had rolled over the bed. The beige paint on the walls looked gray. Even the brown tweed carpet had a gray hue. I reached to the bedside table for my cigarettes, then lay on my back. I lighted up, dragged, coughed hard. The first few drags in the morning always irritated my lungs. I remembered my pleas for a baby, the fatuous singing. *I'm a fool,* I thought, wishing I could blot out last night. Blackouts were terrible, but remembering was worse.

With a groan I pushed up onto my knees, crawled over Gene, and went to the bathroom. I ran the water until it was cold, then bent and drank from the faucet. I scooped up a handful of water and splashed my face. Straightening up, I looked in the mirror. My cheeks were puffy and my watery eyes were rimmed in black, like Dad's when he drank. Under my right eye was a broken vein about half the length of a snail. I had not noticed it before. But it was just like the veins on Dad's face. *They come,* I thought, *from drinking.* I put my finger over the vein and my finger shook.

I turned away and stepped into the hall. I froze. The three children were in Debbie and Donny's bedroom, several feet ahead. They were talking about me.

"Mommy's sick," Debbie said. "I heard her coughing."

"She's always sick," said Donny.

"Why?" Debbie asked.

"Because she drinks."

"Drinking doesn't make *me* sick," Debbie said.

"I wanna drink," said Douglas, who usually craved any food or liquid mentioned in his presence.

"She drinks beer," said Donny. "She drinks it all the time."

"Gimme a drink," said Douglas.

Feeling ill, I clasped my mouth with one hand and my stomach with the other. I darted past the children's door and through the kitchen and down the basement stairs. Midway down I stopped, sank onto a step, pulled my nightgown to my ankles, and drew my knees up to my chin. My teeth chattered.

I wanted to be a lovely mother like my sister Chris. But I hadn't a chance. I'd already ruined my kids. Often lately Donny went into long episodes of blinking. He was unhappy and he blinked to signal the message. Tears came as I pictured his blue eyes blinking. And Debbie sucked her thumb constantly, as if her thumb were her best friend.

I jumped up and ran to the laundry room. Before I consciously understood what I was doing, I had the lid off a tall box of clothes and was rummaging through stacks of sweaters. Inside was an emergency fifth of bourbon. Suddenly I fully realized what I was after and I thought, *Wait. I can't. I never drink in the morning. I won't let myself drink in the morning like Dad.* But then I felt glass—and I lifted out the bottle, uncapped it and drank. As the bourbon went down, I thought, *I'm trailing right after you, Dad—almost walking in your footprints. Pretty soon I'll catch up with you.* "You too, Aunt Red," I whispered.

I took another long swallow, for Dad had always said, "Let's have another one for insurance."

I laughed. I was feeling good. I saw that morning drinking was all right.

I sat on the floor, leaned against the dryer, and placed the bottle between my legs. The floor was concrete, but it did not feel uncomfortable. For a while I studied a curving crack that ran from my knee to the drain. I covered half of the crack with my leg. It was pleasant to sit there with an almost full bottle between my legs.

When the bottle was about a third gone, I heard two sets of footsteps coming down the stairs. Quickly, I put the bourbon in the dryer, gathered an armful of sweaters from the box, and dropped them into the washer. It was Debbie and Donny. I smiled, then poured a cup of soap in with the sweaters.

"I'm doing the laundry," I said. "I noticed all the sweaters were dirty."

"Douglas threw up on the floor," said Debbie. "I made him wipe it up."

"We've been looking for you," said Donny.

"I heard you all playing so I came down to wash."

"Come on upstairs," said Donny. He looked at me seriously, then widened his eyes and blinked. He knew that I was drunk.

"I will. Just as soon as I do a little more washing. Go back upstairs and I'll be right up."

They didn't move. "Go," I commanded. "I'll be up in a second." They left, and I reached into the dryer for the bourbon, then sat on the floor, carefully arranging my leg so that it fully covered the crack.

At some point I slept.

Around noon I awoke with a start. My back ached. Gene was bent over me, his lips pressed tight, his hands gripping my shoulders. He shook me and the bottle rolled from my arm to the drain.

"Get up!" he shouted.

I pushed weakly against the concrete. My hips lifted up a few inches, then fell back to the floor. "I can't," I said. "I'm too tired."

"You're not tired, you're plastered!" he yelled, and his voice seemed harder than the concrete under me. "Get up! You hear me? Get up!"

I pushed with my feet. Again my hips rose up and fell back. "I can't."

He grasped my waist, lifted me, and slung me over his shoulder, as if I were a suit coat. My head spun. I closed my eyes and thought, *This is a dream, this is a dream. You're a lovely person and you always will be.*

We climbed the stairs and went to the bedroom. Gene lowered me onto the bed, rolled me to the middle, then strode away, slamming the door behind him. The house seemed to tremble.

I was too nauseated and distraught to get up, so I spent the rest of Sunday and Sunday night in bed.

Monday morning I awoke to Gene's splashing of water in the bathroom sink. I remembered pieces of Saturday night and Sunday: *The Singing Detective,* Donny's blinking, Gene's "Get up!" Though my stomach was upset, I forced myself out of bed. I was still wearing the flowered nightgown with a V neck that I had put on Saturday night. I started for the bathroom, but my stomach rolled as I went through the doorway, and I leaned against the doorjamb. After a minute I went on. I needed to apologize to Gene and have his forgiveness. I couldn't wait through the day wondering if he hated me. I had to know he loved me.

I opened the bathroom door a crack. "Do you mind if I come in?"

"Yes."

"I'll just be a second."

"Use the bathroom in the basement."

"We've got to talk."

"Later."

I walked in and sat on the edge of the tub. "I can't wait until later."

Gene stood about an arm's length from the tub and was lathering his face with a shaving brush. My eyes were level with the back of his knees. His eyes in the mirror were grim.

"I'm sorry about the weekend," I said.

"Nothing to apologize for. Nothing abnormal. You were completely as usual."

"I was not." Tears came, and I wiped them from my cheeks.

"You were." He paused and rinsed his razor. "I'm not getting into this now. I don't have time."

"Can't you take a minute?"

"No, I've got an early meeting."

"I'm going to quit drinking."

"Later, Muriel."

I shuffled into the kitchen and pulled open the curtains above the sink. A hard rain sent streams of water down the window. I snapped on the overhead light, feeling so low that if the kitchen had blackened and rain had poured from the ceiling, I would not have been surprised.

I was thirsty so I poured a glass of Coke. Then I took eggs, bacon and bread from the refrigerator. If I made breakfast for Gene, which I had not done in years, he would believe that I was sorry and that I meant to quit drinking.

When breakfast was cooked, Gene came in, his London Fog buttoned, his briefcase under his arm. He walked through the smell of the bacon and eggs to the back door. "I'll be home at ten," he said. "I've got class tonight."

"I know."

He reached for the doorknob.

"Wait," I said. "Don't leave yet. I've fixed breakfast."

"I don't have time."

"But it's ready. It's bacon and eggs."

"I told you, I've got an early meeting." He opened the door and closed it quietly, as if to announce that the situation was beyond the anger of a slam. I went to the window and watched him walk through the porch, out the door, along the short sidewalk to the car. I listened to the engine warming up and kept my eyes on the car as it backed past the porch. When I could no longer see it, I leaned my forehead on the window and cried.

Later, I knelt by the front door, zipped Donny's red jacket, and tied the laces of his oxfords. He always forgot to tie them. He wrapped his arms around me, kissed me and left for school.

As he walked down the sidewalk swinging his brown-bag lunch, I called, "Have a good day, darling."

He spun around, smiled, waved.

I felt better.

I read a book to Debbie, and we laughed at Mr. Worm and Mr. Bear. "Could they come live with us?" Debbie asked.

"They're not real," I said.

"I know," said Debbie, "but I like them."

"Then we'll pretend and we'll build them a house."

Douglas, Debbie and I built Mr. Worm and Mr. Bear a house of TinkerToys, and I felt much better.

At noon I left Douglas and Debbie with the TinkerToys, went to the kitchen, and started making peanut butter and jelly sandwiches. The rain had stopped and the sun was sending a circle of light to the floor at my feet. I felt fine now. But along with my lifted spirits rose a resentment of Gene. He had walked past the breakfast. He had brushed aside my apology as carelessly as he would brush aside a fly. I hated him for that. I would show him.

"Lunch is ready," I called to the children. Then, while they came in and sat at the table, I fixed a martini with two olives.

Douglas sipped his milk and stared at the olives. "I want one."

"Okay, honey." I dropped three olives into his milk.

Debbie looked at my martini with concern. "Don't get sick, Mommy."

"Don't worry. Mommy's fine. Would you like some olives?"

"Yes." I put three olives in her glass of milk.

We all drank.

CHAPTER VI

I drank three martinis, then slept. By the time Debbie and Donny got home from school (Debbie was in an afternoon kindergarten class), I was sober, but my head was heavy, my body sluggish.

Late in the afternoon, Mom called. "You're still coming, aren't you?" she asked.

"To?" I had forgotten to what I was coming.

"To dinner."

"Gene'll be at school. He can't come."

"I know that. Muriel, are you all right?"

"I'm fine. I'm just a little sleepy. Of course, I remember I'm coming to dinner." And then I remembered Mom's invitation of a few days ago; dinner would include my sister Chris, her husband, Bruce, and her five children. My sister Ellen would be out with her boyfriend.

"We'll eat at six," Mom said.

I hung up and put on a wool skirt and a yellow blouse, dressing slowly as I still felt lethargic. I was tempted to have a few drinks for energy, but decided against that, because Bruce had a low enough opinion of me already. Though he had never directly expressed his dislike, his occasional nasty comments revealed his feelings. The previous week, at his house he had said, "You smoke too much."

Tonight I wouldn't give him an opportunity to sniff out a few drinks and tell me that I drank too much.

The children and I entered my parents' home through a shed-shaped room which enclosed the stairs between the basement and the kitchen. As we walked up the steps, I smelled ham and cloves and my stomach growled. I had not eaten for two days.

I finished my meal first and Mom said, "You're eating well, Muriel."

"It's good," I said and passed my plate to Dad for seconds on ham and potatoes au gratin.

As my plate went by Bruce, I noted that he didn't say I was a glutton. Actually, thus far he had been congenial, asking about Gene's work and school and talking about his work as a pipe fitter. I almost liked him when he was pleasant.

After dinner Chris washed the dishes and I dried. The steamy dishwater flushed her face, and I noted, as I often did with jealousy, that she was lovely, far lovelier than I. She was slim with dark blond hair, a wide mouth and a long, straight nose. She held her head high and her shoulders back. She had an elegance, a Vassar look. Though I was almost as slim, my shoulders slumped and my forehead was drawn with discouragement.

Chris put her hands into the dishwater. "Isn't it hard with Gene in school?" she said. "You hardly ever see him."

"No, it gives me more freedom."

"Freedom?"

"Free-dom," I said, emphasizing the syllables. "Certain things are easier to do with Gene gone—such as reading. I like to read in peace and quiet."

Chris changed the subject, "I asked you to come to church last week and you said you couldn't. Can you this week?"

Chris and Bruce were church members. Bruce had told Gene and me that he pledged a percentage of his salary to the church. I thought percentage-giving was the mark of an over-religious attitude. And because Bruce wasn't fond of me, I disliked him and his religiousness and his church—even though I knew next to nothing about the church.

"I don't think so," I said. "Gene and I don't like to go that much. He went to too many churches and heard too many doctrines when he was young. He doesn't trust religion."

"For the children's sake, you should both go. Your children should be in Sunday school."

Her tone was prudish and I snapped, "Why?"

"To learn good morals."

"Gene and I teach them morals. Kids don't have to go to

Sunday school to learn morals. Look at the Buddhists and the Jews. Their kids don't go to Sunday school, yet they've got better morals than most kids that do go."

"You're being touchy."

I settled down. "I'm sorry. Maybe we'll try to go next week." I knew we wouldn't try, but I was attempting to compensate for my touchiness.

Later at home, I put the children to bed and waited for Gene. I didn't drink. The desire for revenge was gone; I wanted peace. He came in around ten, and I re-apologized for Saturday and Sunday. With a stolid gaze and polite tone, he said, "That's all right. Forget it."

Be angry, I thought, *or even furious, but don't be so polite and remote.*

"It's been a long day. I'm tired," he said. He kissed my cheek and went to bed.

His rejection angered me. *No more apologizing,* I thought and brought a quart of beer to the basement family room and watched television.

Tuesday night over dinner he was as remote as he had been the night before. I thought, *I've done my best. If he's going to act like a stranger, then I'm going to drink. I won't put up with his self-righteous manner.* Immediately after dinner I took a quart of beer to the family room. When I came up for a second, I saw him on the screened porch leaning over the beer case, evidently counting my empties. I was furious. The spy!

I hate him, I thought, and grabbed another quart from the refrigerator and hurried downstairs.

I worked up a plan to get even with him. On Friday Gene, the children, and I would be driving to Minneapolis with Mom and Dad Canfield for a wedding. The trip had been planned for weeks. We would leave the minute Gene got in from work—that is, everyone but me. I would stay home and have some freedom, drinking in peace without his spying.

On Friday I packed my suitcase as if I were going, made sandwiches, perked coffee, and filled one thermos with coffee and one with lemonade. Late that afternoon after Gene and his parents arrived, we all started across the screened porch on the way to Dad Canfield's car. Before I got to the door, I sank onto a picnic table bench and wrapped my arms around my stomach. I moaned and bent forward.

"What's wrong?" Gene asked.

"I'm nauseated."

Gene looked at me with concern, his first interested look of the week. He came and squatted so that his face was level with mine. "Can I get you something, gal?"

"No," I whispered. With distinct effort I lifted my head. "I think I've got the flu. My head's been aching all day and now my stomach's upset."

"You can't go to Minneapolis in that condition."

"I know."

"We'll stay home. Mom and Dad can go without us."

"Don't do that. The kids have been talking about the trip all day."

"I don't know."

"Really. I'll take aspirin and spend the weekend in bed. It'll be quiet and I'll probably feel better by tomorrow."

"Okay," he said hesitantly. He reached over and stroked my hair and whispered, "I love you, darling. Take care of yourself. We should be home Sunday by early evening."

They left, and I sat on the bench until the noise of Dad Canfield's car faded to a hum. Then I jumped up, trotted to the living room, and turned on the stereo. Stretching my arms like wings, I twirled until the room spun. With a laugh I danced to the kitchen. I took a bottle of gin from the cabinet under the sink and fixed a martini on the rocks.

Around 1:00 a.m. I missed the children. I carried a martini into Debbie and Donny's room and looked at their beds, then walked to Douglas' room. On impulse I snapped out Douglas' light and peered through his window, which overlooked our driveway and my neighbor's kitchen. My neighbor, Erma Howard, was bent over her kitchen table, writing. She wore a green bathrobe. Her brown hair fell in waves to her shoulders. Usually Erma pinned her hair into a bun at the back of her head. *I like it better down,* I thought.

I watched with fascination, feeling godlike, yet she was unaware. Erma pushed a strand of hair from her forehead, glanced toward me and continued writing.

Was it possible that she was a middle-of-the-night writer like me? I laughed and thought about my cookbook. Again Erma looked up from her writing and over at Douglas' window. I frowned. It was obvious the glance meant that she saw me watching her. I had to call and explain.

Holding the martini, I swayed from Douglas' room to the phone which hung on the wall beside the stove. I squinted. There were two phones and two stoves. "Stupid phone," I said.

I set my glass on a front stove burner, hiked up onto the center griddle, and knocked my glass on the floor. Although I was inches from the phone, I had difficulty dialing Erma's number. After what seemed like five minutes, I reached her.

"This is Muriel," I said and laughed with zest to relax her.

"Yes, Muriel?"

"I wasn't watching you from Douglas' window. I was taking his pants to his pants drawer—so don't be nervous."

"I don't understand."

"It's just that I wasn't watching you."

"I see." A long pause. "All right."

"I often do my laundry at night," I said. "A housewife's work is never done." I laughed in conspiracy, for Erma was also a housewife and probably never got her work done. She would understand.

"Why don't you call it a day and go to bed?" she said.

"I guess I should. I was going to wax the kitchen floor, but it can wait until morning."

"I'm sure it can."

"Well—nice talking to you."

"Good night," Erma said.

A brief, but effective call, I thought, and yawned and went to bed.

When I awoke and recalled the conversation with Erma, I blushed. The call had been ridiculous, as screwy as the ones Dad had often tried to put through to Khrushchev. Mom would say, "He's got telephonitis again." When Dad got telephonitis, no one could stop him from dialing anyone.

My call to Erma had been a bad case of telephonitis. It had been nonsensical to call her. With her kitchen light on and Douglas' bedroom light off, she could not have seen me. I couldn't face her again.

Early Saturday evening I opened a can of beer and paced throughout the house, too bored to sit. This was my last free evening, and I needed to go someplace—do something.

I decided I would go to a bar.

This was not a new practice. Sometimes around midnight, when Gene was sound asleep, I would quietly leave the house and go to a bar. A few times, though, he had awakened to find me gone and had had a fit. Then I would stay home for a while until I felt he had settled down.

On one of those excursions I had discovered Mike's Place, a bar on York Street. Tonight it would be best to go there, for Mike's was three miles from my house, far enough away to diminish the odds of meeting a neighbor—like Erma. Not that Erma drank; as far as I knew she didn't. But I felt as if I must be super cautious.

Perched on my bar stool, it was as if I had left Erma and last night, even reality, behind. I loved the unreality; the lights, the smoky haze, the whiny country music. I called to Mike, "I'll have a double bourbon and water."

Mike nodded. A stocky red-headed man on the stool next to mine said, "A mighty big drink for a little girl."

"I don't think so," I said.

"I'll buy the drink," he said.

"All right."

We drank together. His name was Russ. He sold used cars, his voice twanged like that of a rancher, and he straddled his bar stool as if it were a horse and he were a cowboy. He called me honey and little girl, and as I drank more and more, I found myself loving him and telling him that Gene was overperfect—impossible to live up to and with. Amidst the lights and the smoke and the music, it seemed right for Russ to come home with me.

At home we drank until the sun set late Sunday afternoon. I turned on the lamp on the bedside table. I remembered that Gene was coming home soon, but I couldn't relate to the fact. It had the same unreality as Mike's Place.

I became tired about then and I slept.

I awoke feeling as if my head were crushed. I thanked my luck that Russ had left before Gene came home, then I cried, despising myself for what I had done. But I had no time for crying. I had to clean up so that Gene wouldn't suspect that a man had been here. I picked up the slice of pizza, the

Seagram's bottle, the two mugs from which Russ and I had been drinking a mix of bourbon and coffee.

I hurried to the kitchen and snapped on the overhead light. On the counter near the stove was the note. My hands shook as I reached for it and read:

Muriel,
We got home for dinner. I found you and your friend sleeping.
I've got the kids. I won't be coming home.

Gene

Now I had all the time in the world. Gene meant it—he wouldn't come back, for he had high principles. He hated infidelity. And so did I. How could I have done that which I hated? Then the tears came hard. If only I could begin the weekend again, I would go to Minneapolis. Then I wouldn't have gone to Mike's Place and I wouldn't have met Russ and I wouldn't be in this awful trouble.

I threw the note in the garbage bag and paced the kitchen, still crying. *Oh, God*, I thought, *what can I do? Given Gene's high morals, he'll feel compelled to take me to court and divorce me and I'll lose my children. When that happens, I'll want to die.*

The future looked like the Sahara—empty, desolate. Suddenly my head became light. My vision blurred, the floor wavered. I was becoming hysterical. In an automatic response, I reached into the cabinet under the sink for the bourbon, then pulled back my hand. I couldn't drink. I had to keep sober so that I could find Gene and beg him to come home.

I dialed his parents' phone and sank to the floor and leaned against the stove.

Gene answered. "I thought it might be you," he said. His voice was level, but tight.

"I wanted to find you."

"Well, you found me."

"I wanted to tell you I'm sorry."

"Sorry!" he yelled in an explosion of anger. "Sorry—when you've managed to violate everything that marriage stands for!"

His outburst frightened me and I almost dropped the phone. I cried and blew my nose in my bathrobe, then said, "I didn't know what I was doing. I was drunk. I didn't mean to violate anything."

"I don't want to talk about it now. I'm too upset."

"We've got to talk now. You've got to come home. You can't leave me."

"We'll discuss it in the morning."

"Gene—please."

"No." He paused, evidently suppressing his feelings, for when he continued his voice exuded its usual calm tone. "I'll stop before work—around six. Please be up and please be sober."

"You can't divorce me."

"We'll talk in the morning."

He hung up. I closed my eyes and I thought, *Maybe he won't divorce me if I quit drinking. Tomorrow I'll tell him I've stopped. I'll explain that such a thing can't happen again because I won't be drinking again. Maybe he'll understand. Maybe he'll forgive me and come home.*

I perked a pot of coffee and drank two cups of it, then cleaned up the bedroom.

CHAPTER VII

In the morning I washed my face, brushed my teeth, and applied liquid makeup over skin that seemed as pale as the sink. I put on a touch of pink lipstick. There was nothing I could do for my eyes which were red and circled in black. I went to the kitchen, poured a glass of water, sat at the kitchen table, and picked at the nubs on my blue terry cloth robe. I lighted a cigarette. I was terribly nervous. It was a few minutes before six.

At exactly six I heard Gene's car pull into the driveway. I ground out my cigarette and lighted another. When he opened the door, my stomach rolled.

He sat across from me, putting the length of the table between us. He wore a brown suit with pinstripes, a white shirt, a brown-and-green striped tie. He was clean-shaven and smelled of the pine of his after-shave. In my terry robe I felt like a frump.

"Could I get you some coffee?" I asked.

"Please."

After tightening the tie on my robe, I went to the sink, turned on the water, and started to fill the pot. "If you've got to make it, don't bother. I don't have time."

I came back to my chair. "Are the kids okay?"

"They're fine."

"I miss them."

"They miss you, too."

"Please come home," I said, glancing at Gene, then down.

"What went on this weekend?" he barked out in a command.

"I was lonely and . . ." I couldn't continue.

"And?"

"I went to a bar. I—I got drunk and a man came home with me."

"That can't be all."

"No—but I didn't even know him. I was drunk and I didn't know what I was doing."

"That's impossible," he said, his eyebrow high in disbelief.

"I didn't. I was drunk."

He shouted, "You didn't know what you were doing when that man took you in his arms? Are you . . ." All at once Gene's voice broke. I looked up and his eyes were filled with tears. I lowered my eyes. I had never known Gene to cry.

But in a minute he had his composure. "How could you?" he said.

"I don't know," I whispered. "I think I must do things when I'm drinking that I'd never do when I'm sober. I'm really sorry. It'll never happen again because I'm never going to drink again."

"That I don't believe."

"I'm not lying."

"You're always lying." He paused, then said, "Speaking of lies, you didn't have the flu, did you? You made it up so you could spend the weekend with your boyfriend."

"I told you I never met him before. He's not my boyfriend."

"Not likely, Muriel. More likely you met him on one of your midnight forays, then made up the flu so you could spend the weekend together."

Everything was tangled. "That's not true," I said, feeling that same hysteria I had felt the night before. I lifted my glass and it trembled, so I set it down without taking a drink.

Gene watched. My nervousness must have moved him, for he chose to believe me. "Then why did you tell me you had the flu?"

"I was mad at you. I wanted to be alone."

Gene looked through the window above the sink. It was dark and there was nothing to see. "Please come home," I said.

He didn't answer, but kept his eyes on the window. My future hung tenuously in his silence.

Finally he turned to me. "This can't happen again."

"It won't. I told you, I've quit drinking."

"All right," he said, then glanced at his watch and stood. "I've got to get to work."

"The kids?" I said, standing.

"I'll pick them up after work."

He left, but the moment he shut the door I remembered his parents. I ran to the door and pulled it open just as Gene opened the screened porch door. "Wait a minute," I said. "Did you tell your parents any of this?"

"No. I told them we had some problems, but nothing specific."

He started again toward the car and I went inside, relieved that his parents knew nothing. I filled the coffeepot and plugged it in. Then the tension of the last half hour released in a sob and tears.

All day my nerves jumped. The only help would be a drink and that I could not have.

Late in the afternoon Mom phoned. We talked a few minutes, then the back doorbell rang. "Just a second," I said and laid the phone on the stove. It was a magazine salesman with a once-in-a-lifetime offer.

"I think I'll pass," I said to him with some hesitation, for I loved to read.

He capitalized on my hesitation, and I subscribed to two magazines. After shutting the door, I turned and saw the receiver on the stove. I put it to my ear—dead. I dialed Mom.

"What happened to you?" she asked.

"It was a magazine salesman."

"I hung on for fifteen minutes. I was worried."

"I'm sorry, Mom. I forgot."

"Is there something wrong? Do you need me to come?"

"No, I think it's this cold I've got. I got it last night and I don't feel well. Don't worry. I'll be fine by tomorrow."

Mom urged me to call if the cold worsened.

When Gene brought the children home, I hugged and kissed each one. "I missed you, Mommy," Debbie said.

Donny blinked and said, "Are you okay?" I turned away, feeling nauseous.

I couldn't eat dinner.

After dinner when the children were in bed, I went to Gene in the living room where he was reading a marketing text. He closed the book and laid it on the end table beside his chair. "It's been rough for you today, hasn't it, gal?" he said.

"It has. I've been jumpy." I extended my arm and my hand shook. "See?"

Gene took my hand and pulled me onto his lap. I curled up my legs and leaned my head on the back of the chair. He kissed my cheek, then my neck. "Darling," he whispered.

In his love, I cried, releasing the strain of the morning. "Don't cry, darling," Gene said.

"I can't help it."

"I love you."

"I do, too," I said, knowing that any woman except me would thank heaven for a husband like Gene and state emphatically that she loved him. *Why can't I?* I thought.

Gene pulled my shoulders back and looked into my eyes. "Go back to A.A., gal. Give them another try."

"I don't know."

"Please try—for me."

"I'll think about it."

For days I felt jittery and craved a drink. I thought about calling A.A., but calling would mean stating that I was an alcoholic, and I wasn't certain that I was. I saw that I overdrank, but I thought I could muster up my willpower and stay sober. I did not know I was fighting with an addiction.

So I clutched at sobriety. To keep my nerves under control I kept occupied; I scrubbed floors, waxed furniture, baked, talked on the phone.

On the ninth evening of my sobriety, Gene ambled into the kitchen, set his coffee mug in the sink, yawned, and rubbed his eyes. "I can't study anymore. My eyes are burning." He had a marketing exam the following evening.

I was kneeling on the floor, spraying the cabinet under the sink with wax. "Do you know it pretty well?"

"Pretty well. I should be all right."

He bent and kissed the top of my head. "I'm heading to bed. Why don't you call it quits and come along?"

"I'll be in soon."

As I rubbed the wax, I considered the B.S. Gene had and

the M.B.A. he would soon have. All that education guaranteed success. But I, a college dropout, had about as much potential as my waxing cloth. If only I had finished college and had gone on to an advertising career.

I imagined I were working on the Procter & Gamble account, composing an ad for Jif peanut butter. I pictured a boy of ten turning the lid on a Jif jar that was almost as tall as he. Behind him a chorus sang, "When Johnny gets a whiff of the Jif." *Terrific,* I thought. *A masterful ad. But of no application.* I had a trapped-in-the-kitchen talent.

I felt terrible. There was my squelched talent, but it was as a breeze to a hurricane. The real problem was going through each miserable day sober. That was killing me.

I was about to crumble or snap.

So I scooted along the floor to the cabinet under the sink and I reached for the bourbon bottle, lifted it, drank. And then I thought, *What am I doing? If Gene walked in and found me, he'd have a fit.*

But in a moment the bourbon settled and I thought, *a drink or two couldn't hurt anybody and a drink or two couldn't hurt me.* And chances were one in two million that Gene would get up and come to the kitchen. He was exhausted.

Later when the bottle was nearly empty, I tilted back on a kitchen chair, propped my feet against the table, and made plans: In the morning I would hire a baby-sitter, get on the Aurora & Elgin train and get off at the Loop. There I would apply for a job as an ad executive. A person like me would have no trouble landing a job like that.

I tipped forward, jumped up, and pulled the phone directory from atop the refrigerator. I had to call Russ with my spectacular news. He liked me, maybe even loved me. He would want to celebrate. I dialed, Russ answered, and I blurted out, "You should meet me at Mike's. We should celebrate."

"Celebrate what? Who is this?" he said. He sounded sleepy, as if I had awakened him.

"Muriel." Hurt that he didn't know who I was, I asked, "Couldn't you recognize my voice?"

"At one in the morning?"

"What about Mike's? Can you go?"

"No. It's late. I've got to work tomorrow."

His cool reception of my celebration upset me. "I thought you liked me."

"I do."

"Then let's go."

"I'm not going. I'm not going to take a chance on getting mixed up with your husband."

"We'll be careful."

"No, little girl."

"You're a coward!" I shouted and banged down the receiver, hating Russ, the spineless, sleepy worm. At least I had a few guts in me and wasn't a person like him.

Gene wasn't a person like Russ either. He had guts, because obviously he had intimidated Russ.

"Hey, Gene!" I screamed and started into the hall toward our bedroom. "Wake up! Wait'll you hear what just happened." I swayed into the bedroom and flipped on the ceiling light. "Wake up! It's me."

Gene blinked and pushed himself up on his elbows. "What's wrong?" he asked.

"It's Russ. That man you don't like. He's a coward. You intimidated him."

Gene studied my face. His eyes turned cold and he roared, "You're drunk!"

I stepped back from his anger and leaned against the closet door. "I'm not very drunk. I only drank a little."

"Enough! Shut up! Don't tell me!" he yelled. Then like lightning he sat and swung his legs over the side of the bed.

He looked as if he were about to storm from the room. I dropped into his lap and said, "I'm trying to tell you you're a better man than Russ. He's a coward. Don't you hear? I just about love you. I don't love Russ."

Gene gave me a stunned look. In a monotone he said, "You are plastered out of your mind. You are behaving like a mad woman. Either you cannot, or you choose not to, stop drinking. But you"—his voice rose—"*will* stop drinking. You are going to see our doctor tomorrow."

"I don't want to. I'm not sick."

Now Gene's voice was loud. "You *are* sick. You *will* see Dr. Thompson."

I felt dizzy. *All right,* I thought. The rest, if there was any more, was a blank.

In the morning Gene phoned. "I just called Dr. Thompson's office. You've got an appointment at two."

"I'm sorry about last night. It won't happen again."

"Excuse me if I have trouble with that. Just go to the doctor."

"I don't think I need a doctor for this."

"You do. Don't argue. You're going."

He was cornering me. I couldn't chance his taking the children and leaving. "All right," I said.

I remembered his marketing exam. "Good luck on your test."

"I'll need it."

At Dr. Thompson's office a nurse opened the door leading to a string of examination rooms. She called my name, and led me down a long hall and into a small room. "The doctor will be with you in a minute," she said and left. I took a seat next to a white supply cabinet. I was nervous. To keep my thoughts away from the reason for the appointment, I studied the instruments, the white walls, the white floor, the picture on the wall of a sky-full of migrating birds. I pulled at my skirt and traced its green checks with my finger. Even though I tried to think about the checks, I found myself staring at the supply cabinet and wishing it contained a bottle of bourbon. *One sip,* I thought, *and my nerves would settle down.*

Just then the door swung open and Dr. Thompson came in, smiling. He was about seventy with a boyish smooth face and clear blue eyes behind thick bifocals. He had been my doctor and my parents' doctor for twenty years. I didn't smile in return, for I was feeling ashamed. How could I possibly tell him I was an out-of-control drinker?

Dr. Thompson pulled up a chair and sat opposite me with his knees inches from mine. "How's your mom?"

"Fine."

"Your dad's knee?"

Frequently Dad's knee swelled and throbbed, a result of a high school football injury. "He's been limping lately."

Dr. Thompson nodded. "And Gene and the children?"

"Fine."

"And you?"

"I'm—" Then I spoke so fast that I almost believed someone else were speaking. "I'm drinking too much."

Dr. Thompson nodded; his eyes were warm. Whether it was his warmth or whether it was because I had said the worst of it, I quickly went on.

"I drink every night and sometimes during the day. I shake all morning. I black out several nights a week. I have diarrhea all day. I'm nervous all the time. I spend money on liquor that should be spent on the children. I yell at them. I'm not a good mother."

I paused, remembering the long list of alcoholics in the family. I saw that my name belonged on the list, but I didn't want it there. I wanted sobriety, for myself, for the person I might yet be.

I continued. "I never meant to become a drinker, but I am. I've got to stop." While speaking, I had forgotten my shame, but now it came back as I added, "I'm out of control." I started to cry.

Dr. Thompson reached into the supply cabinet, took out a tissue, and handed it to me. While I blew my nose, he leaned back in his chair, as if to give us a better perspective. "In a sense you're not in control. You're addicted."

"I'm an alcoholic."

"Yes." He explained that abstinence was the only course, A.A. the best method.

"I've tried A.A. It didn't work."

"It works, Muriel. Maybe you weren't ready then." He pulled a prescription pad from his pocket. "I'm giving you the name and number of an A.A. member. I want you to call her."

I agreed to call, and as I stood to leave, Dr. Thompson said, "Call in a week or so and let me know how you're doing."

CHAPTER VIII

Helen, my prescription from Dr. Thompson, was driving me to her A.A. meeting in Villa Park, a suburb adjacent to Elmhurst. A heavy woman with chubby fingers, she was gesturing and explaining that the meeting would be in Johnny's basement. My attention was focused mostly on my doubts about going. In the confines of Gene's ultimatum and Dr. Thompson's office, I had been certain I had a severe drinking problem. Now I wasn't so sure.

When we got to Johnny's long, tan ranch-style house, Helen led me around the back, down a flight of stairs, and into the basement—a drab, depressing place. The floor was painted battleship gray, and the walls were poured concrete. A Ping-Pong table at one end of the room, under a bare light bulb, held a fifty-cup coffeepot and stacks of coffee cups. At the other end about twenty men and women sat in a circle. Above them a fluorescent tube flickered, almost burned out. Smoke hovered around the tube and clouded the room. In the smoky, dim, pulsing light, I had the same surreal feeling I often had in taverns. And for a moment I was disoriented, feeling as if I were not really me and not really at an A.A. meeting.

Helen took a seat and I sat beside her. "Which one is Johnny?" I asked.

"Over there." Helen pointed to a man of about sixty-five with a mound of a stomach and a bald head.

She introduced me to the A.A. members sitting beside us. Then, as chairwoman, she started the meeting. The discussion subject was "stinking thinking," an A.A. coinage that I took to

78

mean thoughts of self-pity that endanger an alcoholic's sobriety. Helen skipped around the group asking for comments,
unnerving to me, for while each person spoke, I thought, *Oh,
no, this time it'll be me.* I was hearing little that was said and
leaned over and whispered to Helen, "Please don't call on
me." She nodded. Now I could listen.

When about half the members had commented, Helen
called on Pat, an attractive woman with an unseasonable tan
and cropped brown hair that peaked at the crown. She was tall
and with her length and hair she looked like a stretched-out
pixie. She looked familiar. Who was she? Then with a start I
remembered that she was Pat Lovett, a classmate from York
Community High School. She had been an acquaintance, not
a friend. I had not had friends like Pat Lovett, who had been a
"hood"—one of the girls who smoked in the rest room, wore a
black leather jacket, drew on oversized lips with a blazing red
lipstick. She was the kind of girl one might expect to wind up
in A.A. But not me. So what was I doing here with her? How
could this have happened?

Pat said that three years ago, shortly after she came to
A.A., she fought with her husband, developed "stinking
thinking," and got drunk. "A *long* drunk," she said. "It took
me eight weeks to get off the liquor. But by the grace of God I
got back to A.A. And by His grace, I'm sober today." She did
not stutter or search for words, as I expected a person like she
might. In fact, to my surprise she spoke fluently and was a far
better speaker than I.

I was impressed. She had three years of sobriety behind
her. I had three days.

To close the meeting, we all stood and recited the Lord's
Prayer. I spoke in a whisper.

After the prayer, Helen and I, along with most of the
group, picked up our chairs, brought them to the Ping-Pong
table, and drank coffee. Several of the people introduced
themselves. Then Pat came. "I know I know you," she said.

"We both went to York," I said.

"Of course," she said, then told me she remembered me as
a quiet girl, a good student, a member of the girls' choir. She
was as surprised as I that I had come from that to A.A.

"How do you do it?" I asked. "How do you stay sober? I
wanted a drink coming over. I want one now."

"I do it a day, sometimes an hour, sometimes a minute at a time."

"My doctor said alcoholics have to abstain. All those minutes of yours are adding up to forever."

"I don't think in those terms."

"I do."

"In A.A. we stay sober for today, not for tomorrow."

I became quiet and wondered how I could stay sober today and then tomorrow, which would be a today, and on and on through a forever of todays. Rightly interpreting my silence to mean I had some doubt about the A.A. approach, Pat said, "It works."

"It has for you, anyway."

"It will for you. You don't have to do it alone. God will help you."

"Maybe."

"Just ask Him."

"I don't know. Maybe I will." But I wasn't planning to, because God, if He did exist, had never responded to one of my prayers and I doubted that He ever would.

"You need a sponsor, too," Pat said.

"A sponsor?"

"Someone you can call on to help you work through the A.A. steps to recovery."

Pat took my phone number and said she would call in the morning. Several minutes later Helen and I left.

At home I found Gene in the living room studying marketing. As I sat on the couch, he closed the book. "How was it?" he asked.

"I didn't mind it. It's in a gloomy basement, but the people are nice."

"You know I'm behind you in this."

"You pushed me into it!" I snapped.

"I pushed because I care about you."

The caring he expressed was in his eyes and I softened. "Do you think I can make it?" I asked.

"You can make it, gal."

"I'm not so sure."

"I am."

CHAPTER IX

In the morning I unearthed *Alcoholics Anonymous* from my sweater drawer. I had kept the book all these years as a gauge, occasionally taking it out and reading and deciding that I wasn't an alcoholic. Reassured, I would re-hide the book. It had to be hidden, for if another should see it, she would wonder why I owned the book and conclude I had a drinking problem. And she would think me a misfit, one who walked a crooked road, leaning on a cracked cane.

It was essential that others view me as sober and sound, for if they so perceived me, then maybe I was all right.

That morning, though, I used the book not as a gauge, but as a text. I found the twelve suggested steps for recovery from alcoholism, the core of the A.A. program:

1. We admitted we were powerless over alcohol—that our lives had become unmanageable.
2. Came to believe that a Power greater than ourselves could restore us to sanity.
3. Made a decision to turn our will and our lives over to the care of God *as we understood Him.*
4. Made a searching and fearless moral inventory of ourselves.
5. Admitted to God, to ourselves, and to another human being the exact nature of our wrongs.
6. Were entirely ready to have God remove all these defects of character.
7. Humbly asked Him to remove our shortcomings.
8. Made a list of all persons we had harmed, and became willing to make amends to them all.

9. Made direct amends to such people wherever possible, except when to do so would injure them or others.
10. Continued to take personal inventory and when we were wrong promptly admitted it.
11. Sought through prayer and meditation to improve our conscious contact with God *as we understood Him,* praying only for knowledge of His will for us and the power to carry that out.
12. Having had a spiritual awakening as the result of these steps, we tried to carry this message to alcoholics, and to practice these principles in all our affairs.[5]

The Twelve Steps upset me; they were religious and I was not. I skimmed back through them and counted: six mentioned God or Power or Him. And the entire God-emphasis culminated in step twelve with a spiritual awakening. How could I, who had no relationship with God or a Power, work through such steps? Too troubled to wait for Pat to phone me, I phoned her and explained my problem.

According to Pat, the steps were designed so that anyone with any conception of God could work through them. Hadn't I noticed, she asked, that the steps did not require one to view God as a Christian God, but only to view Him as one could best understand Him? The purpose of the spiritual emphasis was to lift the alcoholic's gaze up and away from himself and onto a will or power or God, the someone or something in this universe greater than he; for all alcoholics were self-centered and self-willed.

"But," she said, "in my opinion it's much better to develop a relationship with the Christian God, for that leads to complete serenity."

Except when drunk, I had never had serenity. I had always wanted it. "How do I develop a relationship with God?"

"Pray," she said. "Ask God to help you. Soon you'll know He's listening."

I agreed to pray, then asked Pat to be my sponsor. She accepted.

After our conversation, I went to my bedroom; leaving the

---

[5]Alcoholics Anonymous World Services, Inc., *Alcoholics Anonymous,* pp. 59-60. The Twelve Steps reprinted with permission of Alcoholics Anonymous World Services, Inc.

door ajar, I knelt beside the bed. "Dear God or Higher Power," I said, "please help me. Please keep me away from liquor." As I was about to stand, I heard light steps coming across the carpet. It was Debbie with her teddy bear in her arms.

"Who were you talking to?" she asked and widened her eyes into a puzzled expression.

"You heard?"

"I was in the doorway."

"I was talking to God. I was praying."

"What's praying?"

I explained as I thought a mother should. "When a person prays, he talks to God. God lives above us in a place called heaven. He's the Father of everyone in the world. Any time we want, we can pray and ask Him for help. He loves us."

"Does He love me?" Debbie asked.

"Yes."

She knelt beside me and put her teddy bear on the bed and her hands in her lap. "I love You, too, God," she said.

I cried and whispered, so softly that my words were almost a thought, "I want to love You, too."

That night Gene came home from school with a half-gallon of chocolate-marshmallow ice cream and some good news. Even though tired from that last episode with me, he had come through with an 88% on his marketing exam.

"I'm glad," I said. "I felt bad about making you tired."

"Forget it. It's done with and it came out fine."

He began to scoop ice cream into bowls, and I told him about the A.A. steps to recovery and my prayer. "To make it in A.A., I need to develop spiritually."

"It sounds like it," said Gene.

"Do you ever pray?"

"Never."

"You must. Everyone does once in awhile."

"I don't and I don't plan to."

"Don't you ever need help?"

"I take care of myself."

That he did. He was entirely self-sufficient and had taken on not just himself but me as well.

"I can't seem to take care of myself."

Gene handed me a bowl. He gave me a penetrating look. "Then I think you should pray," he said.

I did pray daily to God as I understood Him, a God that was as substantial as the fog in the morning. But I prayed and hoped that understanding and substance would come. And I talked to Pat daily, went to Johnny's basement weekly, went to a Thursday afternoon A.A. meeting, and read *Alcoholics Anonymous*. I tried to accept the first two steps of the Twelve Steps.

But through it, I was miserable, because I couldn't shake the thought that I was headed off into a forever of nondrinking.

I had no serenity and I craved alcohol.

Then one day in mid-November, three weeks after I had entered A.A., I noted the business hours on the door of the liquor store on Spring Road. The next day I noted them again. *Just wondering*, I thought. *No harm in wondering*. After all, when a person had traded at a store for years, it was natural to glance at the hours. It was like a habit. The following day I went inside and bought a case of beer and a bottle of bourbon. But that didn't mean I would be getting drunk and quitting A.A. It simply meant I would have a drink or two that night and a drink or two now and then.

That night after Gene went to bed, I got a champagne glass, filled it with bourbon, and took it to the living room. It did not seem strange to be drinking uncut bourbon from a champagne glass; instead, it felt wonderful, like a celebration. After the bourbon was down, I lay on the carpet with my head parallel to the fireplace. I felt the living room corners round, the lamplight soften, the carpet become a mattress. I had serenity.

I refilled the glass.

Before long I was lonely in my serenity, and I wanted to share it with Ellen, my twenty-year-old sister. Ellen lived with Mom and Dad, and was a secretary. Often she came on the spur of the moment to drink with me. Or to chauffeur me from bar to bar when I had the urge to go but was too drunk to drive.

I dialed and Ellen answered. "Can you come for a drink?" I asked.

"I thought you weren't drinking. Too many calories or something like that."

"Not really, I'm thin enough. Come on over."

"You tend to forget that I work."

"Bring your clothes. You can spend the night."

"Oh, all right."

While I waited for Ellen, I felt the usual regret at having asked her over. For I was the one who had started her into drinking. I had given her champagne when she was twelve, started her on beer when she was sixteen, begun her on highballs at eighteen. Now she was quickly developing a problem with alcohol.

Yet could I really blame myself that she liked to drink? Didn't a person have control over her own destiny?

I didn't know, but I did know that Gene hated her drinking almost as much as he hated mine. In addition, he hated that Ellen had a weak stomach and often vomited on the carpet or a bed after drinking. On noting one of Ellen's accidents, Gene's usual comment was, "Keep your blasted sister out of this house."

Now I heard a squeak and turned. It was Ellen, quietly pushing open the front door, wisely not ringing the bell and waking Gene.

Ellen was five feet two, small-boned, and slim with round dark eyes and thick brown hair. She was quite pretty. After she got a bourbon and water, she stretched out on the carpet, belly down, and scrutinized me. "Why don't you get another glass and mix some ice and water in with your bourbon?" she snapped. "At the rate you're going, you won't be worth six cents, and I'll have wasted my time coming over."

"I'll be all right."

"You will not." She jumped up, took the champagne glass and returned with a water glass, in it a highball like hers.

"That wasn't necessary," I said.

"It was," she said and dropped to the floor and rolled back onto her stomach.

"How's Harry?" I asked. Ellen loved Harry, her boyfriend now for three weeks. We discussed why Mom disliked him.

"Harry's special," Ellen declared.

"Very," I said. Then becoming bored with Harry and wanting some excitement, I said, "Let's go to Mike's."

"No. I told you before, I've got to work tomorrow." In a sweep she sat, then took a long drink and said, "I need your advice. Harry wants me to lend him money for a down payment on a car. Do you think I should?"

"If it were me and I loved him, I'd give it to him."

At first Ellen was reluctant to part with her five hundred dollars, but after a few drinks she came around to my point of view. She then yawned and said, "I'm tired. I'm going to bed. Douglas' room, right?"

In the past she usually slept in Douglas' room on the spare double bed, but tonight, although not able to define why, I felt that would be unwise. "No. I'll move Donny and Debbie into Douglas' room, and you and I can sleep in their beds."

"It's stupid to wake them up."

Suddenly I understood my reason. "I've got to. I can't sleep with Gene. He'll smell the liquor and have a fit."

She then helped me move Donny and Debbie into Douglas' room.

Debbie woke me in the morning. "I'm hungry, Mommy."

My head pounded. It was murder to open my eyes, but I got up and headed along the hall toward the kitchen. Debbie jumped along beside me. "Why'd you sleep in my room?" she asked. "Why did Donny and I sleep in Douglas' room?"

"Because Aunt Ellen spent the night and wanted to sleep with me."

"Why didn't she sleep in Douglas' room?"

"Because."

"Why?"

"Because."

Her mouth opened. One more "why" would take off the top of my aching head. "That's enough!" I snapped.

"Can I get out the cereal?" she asked.

"Yes—please."

While she set the cereal and bowls on the table, I set out a carton of milk, three glasses of orange juice, and called Donny and Douglas. Just as they began eating, the phone rang. It was Gene.

His voice crackled as he said, "You were dead to the world this morning."

"What do you mean?"

"I mean I tried to wake you and I couldn't."

"I was tired."

He snapped at me as I had snapped at Debbie, "Enough. I

shook you and you were passed out."

"I wasn't. I must have been exhausted."

"Muriel, what went on here last night?" he barked.

Quickly I thought through my situation. Since Gene and Ellen probably left for work at about the same time, he would know she had spent the night. But he couldn't possibly know I had been drinking. He had been asleep. I had heard him snoring. I said, "Ellen was here, but nothing went on."

"I'm trying to give you a chance to explain this."

"Explain what?"

"What went on!" he yelled.

"Nothing. Believe me—nothing."

"Really? Nothing?" His voice drove hard. "Then why did I wake up and find your sister in my bed? She *did not* get there via the U.S. mail. She *did not* float down from a cloud. What was she doing there?"

I was a wreck, not knowing how Ellen had gotten to our bed and not able to think up an on-the-spot plausible explanation. But I had to; this episode could be the final straw. I stalled. "I don't know. She must've got there by mistake."

"By mistake! Impossible. A better explanation is that you and Ellen tore into the booze and she got too plastered to know where she slept."

I gave up. "Maybe you're right."

"Maybe I'm right!"

"I'm sorry it happened."

"You were plastered, too." It was a statement, not a question.

"Yes."

He said nothing and I added, "I'm trying not to drink. The A.A.'s say this can happen. They call it a slip. I promise I'm trying."

"Last night was trying?" he said with sarcasm.

"Be fair."

"I'm too fair. Nobody should be this fair."

"Please give me a chance."

A long pause. "All right, Muriel. I'll give you your chance."

He hung up and I called Ellen at her office. "What happened last night?" I asked.

"Do you mean me being in bed with Gene?"

"Yes, I'm in trouble."

"I don't know how I got there."

I quizzed Ellen, but she was bewildered. "Is he mad?" she asked.

"Very. You can't do that again."

"Who'd want to do that again?" she said with annoyance. Her phone buzzed. "I'll talk to you later."

"Wait one second. I can't drink anymore."

"Because of me?"

"No, because of everything."

CHAPTER X

It was a Thursday afternoon in mid-December, hours before the A.A. meeting in Johnny's basement. I opened the refrigerator, poured a glass of beer, almost poured it down the drain. These last weeks I was finding that grasping sobriety was as difficult as hopping a freight at full throttle. I had been in a pattern of drinking a few days, apologizing, sobering up a few days, attending Johnny's A.A. meeting. I always went because Gene needed to see that I was trying. For he was, as promised, giving me a chance. But he was watching and waiting, and I kept thinking, *If I don't make it soon he'll leave.*

But I couldn't pour out the beer. And I drank it and several others, until suddenly I was a wonderful person, the kind of person who could rush to the Loop and find a job as an executive in an advertising agency.

I felt great and wanted to feel greater, but because Gene was waiting and watching I had to sober myself up and get to the meeting.

I put on the coffeepot.

By the time I got into our Volkswagen and started plowing through a slushy snow toward Johnny's, I was sober. Large snowflakes splashed against the windshield, blurring visibility ahead. I strained to see. *Lousy, rotten night to be out,* I thought. Anybody else in any other situation could have stayed home.

The meeting opened with the Serenity Prayer. As usual I recited it absently. To me the prayer was simply a graceful

89

string of words. After praying, the group discussed acceptance—accept yourself, accept your alcoholism, accept your circumstances. I listened apathetically and thought, *As soon as this meeting's over, I'm going home and having a drink.*

The meeting closed and I headed for my coat. Pat intercepted me and touched my arm.

"How's it going?" she said.

"Fine."

I liked Pat. We talked daily and she knew that I drank. I told her most of my problems. But without an explanation I said, "I'm not staying for coffee." She would tell me that nothing warranted a drink and I wasn't up to telling her that nothing could keep me from one.

"Why not?" she asked and gave me a worried look. "You always stay for coffee."

I had to give her an explanation. "Gene's expecting me. He doesn't like me driving in this weather. He gets nervous about me. I promised him I'd come right home."

"Well, call in the morning," she said.

I went to my coat at the wall peg. I put it on and bent to pull on my boots. Just then I heard Johnny call, "Wait."

I straightened up. Johnny was plodding toward me, as if the roll of fat around his middle were weighting him to the floor. I tapped my foot impatiently. I hated being delayed by long-winded Johnny. He would get a person in a corner and go off into a discourse on one of the twelve steps or some concept that popped into his mind. I could see a speech in his eyes.

And there was. While I fidgeted, he told me at great length that if I continued slipping and sobering up, I would drive myself nuts. "Literally nuts," he said. "I'm not kidding. This happens all the time. People come in and they fool around with the program like you do and they go nuts. You will literally drive yourself crazy."

Johnny was scaring me. I remembered Mary, whose mind had become so scrambled that she had been committed to Elgin. *I wasn't headed there,* I thought—*or was I?* Several times lately I had seen lightning flashing across the bedroom. Of course, I had been sobering up and I was nervous, but what was lightning doing in the bedroom?

And I was becoming absentminded. Twice that month I had parked a full grocery cart at the curb fronting the A & P and had driven home without picking up the bags.

And there were the knives. Recently while chopping an onion, I thought, *Maybe I could take a knife like this and stab someone. Who? Why?* I thought wildly and dropped the knife in the sink and broke out into a cold sweat. I was terrified. Now every time I pulled open the knife drawer, I trembled and my hands perspired. So I avoided knives and mainly cooked foods that didn't require chopping.

Maybe I wasn't quite all right, but I wasn't going to think about that.

And I certainly wasn't going to share my worries with Johnny, because he'd go on until midnight about my awful future. "I'm okay," I said. "When I have a slip, I don't drink much. Hardly a drop."

"Have it your way, Muriel, but you might find you've had it your way one day too long."

"Well, thanks anyhow," I said. "Really, I'm okay. I'm doing pretty well."

I left.

Outside the snow had stopped, the roads had been plowed, snow lay heavy on the trees and the yards. I looked up. The sky had cleared and points of silver starlight shone down on the snow-covered trees.

I scraped the snow from the windshield and pulled away from Johnny's curb. I did not know I was beginning the most important ride of my life.

I did know that Johnny's comments had rattled me. And the miserable months that had preceded tonight had almost done me in. I was tired of trying to stay sober. The best solution to it all was to drive to Georgia and never come back. I'd start a new life down there and I'd be happy. Because I wasn't a floozy. I wasn't heading for Mary's Elgin.

But even as I planned the escape, I was beginning to remember a line of the Serenity Prayer: "God grant me the serenity to accept the things I cannot change." Some power within the words broke into me, and showed me I wasn't accepting my life, myself, indeed the greatest thing I could not change—my alcoholism. If I didn't, I would soon lose Gene, the children, and any chance at serenity.

I knew I had come to my bottom. One step lower would be one step too far. From there I wouldn't be able to reach toward the life I wanted to have, the person I wanted to be.

I accepted the fact that I would not drink today and tomorrow. I determined to learn how to break forever into a day at a time. In effect, I took step one of the Twelve Steps. I went on and took step two. But I didn't have enough belief to take step three. I couldn't turn my will over to God.

As I turned onto Spring Road and heard snow splash out from the tires and saw the snow on the steeple of the church and the stars hanging about the steeple like silver lamps, I felt close to God as I understood Him. "God," I prayed, "help me believe in You."

It was the beginning of my sobriety.

CHAPTER XI

I stayed sober. The lightning left the bedroom, I didn't forget my grocery bags at the store. Occasionally I took a knife from the drawer, held it and dropped it back in with trembling hands. But today in January, three weeks after the snowy ride, I was chopping an onion for gravy. My hands perspired but I was determined to get over this fear. And I was determined to stay sober, even though I often craved a drink all day.

I put the chopped onion in the gravy on the stove and turned just as Gene came in from work. He threw his coat on a chair, leaned against the sink, and said, "I've got some good news." He was smiling.

"What?" I said, taking a seat at the table.

"I've been offered a job in Cincinnati as a project engineer in the engineering division. (Procter & Gamble's headquarters is in Cincinnati.) It's a good opportunity. I've got a better chance to advance in the engineering division than in a plant."

"Why?"

"Because I'm a civil engineer. My interest is more in managing projects and construction than in managing production."

"What would you become in the engineering division?"

"I'd start as an engineer and then become a group leader and then a section head, then a department head. That's far enough ahead to look."

"What's the highest job there?"

"Director of Engineering."

"Would you ever make that?"

"How do I know?"

I thought he would.

He came and sat across from me. "I told my boss I'd talk it over with you. There's something we need to consider. I'm worried about you leaving your A.A. group."

I didn't know what to say. I didn't want to stand in the way of a job that would lead to Gene's success. His success would be my success, and I would think well of myself. "I think I could leave," I said.

"But how would you feel about leaving?"

"I'd miss them."

"You're not getting at what I want to know. Would it cause you to drink?"

"I don't think so." I thought about Mike's Place and the liquor store down the street with its business hours on the door. "Maybe it'll be easier to stay sober there," I said. "I mean, I won't be near certain places that remind me of drinking."

"You think you might be better off there?"

"I think so."

"Should I tell my boss we'll go?"

"Yes."

"You're sure?"

"I'm sure."

"We'll have to take a house-hunting trip."

"When?"

"In a few days. They need the job filled as soon as possible."

We flew to Cincinnati and contacted Mrs. Smith, a real estate agent. A tall and lean woman, she was impressive in her gray suit with its straight lines and even seams that had no straggling threads. For hours, while we climbed in and out of her Cadillac, she chatted about property values, interest rates, the Cincinnati Reds, and Rookwood pottery. "It was made in Cincinnati until the early 1940s," she said.

By the time we pulled up before a tan brick ranch-style house which hugged the top of a hill, I was tired and hoping this would be "it." We climbed the steep driveway, then followed Mrs. Smith into the house, through the seven rooms, and out onto the patio, all in one relatively unbroken line, as the house had no basement. Smoothly, Mrs. Smith pulled off her white gloves, lighted a cigarette, pointed, and said, "Beyond the blackberry canes you'll notice a cemetery. In my opinion it's far more desirable to border a quiet cemetery than a busy golf course."

It had begun to drizzle, and I peered through the mist. In the cemetery hundreds of tombstones rose from limp, snow-patched grass. And in front of the tombstones, faded plastic flowers bloomed.

Gene said, "I like the privacy."

I glanced back at the kitchen window, an expanse of glass overlooking the cemetery—my everyday view if we rented the place. "I don't like this kind of privacy."

"Why?"

"Because . . ." How could I tell Gene in front of suave Mrs. Smith that I didn't want to be reminded of death? I continued, "Because I like being closer to stores. I'll have to drive all over the place to get anywhere."

"You're only a mile and a half from shopping," said Mrs. Smith, then dropped her cigarette on the patio and tapped it out with her toe. She lowered her voice and gave Gene a level look. "The rent's only a hundred and fifty."

"Hear that?" Gene said.

"I still don't think so."

"I think we should take it."

We argued quietly for a few moments.

"I like this rent," Gene insisted finally.

"I don't know," I said, starting to give in. This was the cheapest rent we had encountered—and I was tired. I couldn't look at another house. "Okay. Let's take it."

Mrs. Smith signaled her approval with a smile, and we went back to the office and signed the lease. The next morning we flew home.

A few weeks later, the day before the movers came, I went to my last meeting in Johnny's basement. All through the meeting, it seemed that leaving them wouldn't be difficult, but as I stood at the stairway with my coat zipped and mittens on saying good-bye to Pat, I started to cry.

"You gave me my start," I said, feeling love for her.

"You did it yourself. You're the one who came. You're the one who kept coming back."

"But you helped me come back. I'll miss you."

Pat nodded. "I'll miss you."

I took one last look at the circle of chairs and the Ping-Pong table, then rushed up the stairs, blind with tears.

I didn't think I could stay sober in Cincinnati.

Just before we left for Cincinnati, we stopped to see my parents, and I had a moment alone with Ellen in the living room. "Be sure to come visit some weekend," I told her. "Bring Harry."

"I've about had it with Harry."

"I thought you loved him."

"He's lazy. Last night he was too tired to go out. The night before he showed up an hour late."

Until that moment, I had forgotten that I had advised her to give Harry a car down payment. "Did you give Harry your money?"

"No. The next day it seemed like a bad idea."

"It was." Then feeling concern about her hard drinking, I said, "Take it easy. Watch the drinks."

"I do. I'm perfectly fine," she said, just as I had said, many times.

In Cincinnati at the Carrousel Inn, I was sitting in my nightgown, trying to read the *Cincinnati Enquirer*. But the print was blurring in my tears. We had checked in several hours before, awaiting our furniture, which would arrive in the morning. It was 11:00 p.m., and Gene and the children had just fallen asleep.

The room was attractive and bright, but it seemed bleak to me. I missed Mom and Dad and Pat and was too upset to sleep. *If only I were in Elmhurst instead of Cincinnati,* I thought. Here there were no friends, no family, no Johnny's basement, no certainty about anything—the future like rough air. I was afraid of it. I needed a smooth future. And there was only one way to it—a drink. A drink had always smoothed out everything.

I lost sight of Gene's chance of success in the engineering division and saw instead the liquor store on Spring Road with the business hours lettered in black. I imagined myself walking in and searching the rows of bottles for the weekly special.

I had to have a drink.

But I didn't want Gene to know that.

I took off my nightgown, not thinking I was going to go out to drink but thinking, *I'm taking off my nightgown.* I put on slacks and a sweater, brushed my hair, powdered my nose. *I'm getting dressed,* I thought. I pulled my coat from the hanger, picked up my purse, opened the door, and shut it without a sound. *Gene will never know I've stepped out.* I inhaled the chilly air and admitted it: *I'm going out for a drink.*

Though the night was cold, the sky was clear with hundreds of stars twinkling in the distance. It seemed that the stars in Elmhurst had been nearer.

I hurried into our Volkswagen and backed away. About a mile down the road I found a bar with a bright blue and red neon sign. I pulled around the back and parked. I moved my hand to open the door, then stopped, remembering I had spent my last dollar that afternoon at the drugstore. But I was certain I had enough change for a drink or two. Reaching into my purse, I felt around—nothing. I remembered the time at the navy apartment when I had been looking for change for beer. *I've got lousy luck with money,* I thought.

A streetlight at the corner of the lot threw dim light toward the car. I could barely see and snapped on the dome light, turned my purse upside down, and shook it over the seat. Twenty-five cents fell to the seat, enough for a cup of coffee, but far short of the price of a drink.

Blasted luck. Now I would have to drive back. At the motel I eased open the door and tiptoed to Gene's wallet on the bed-side table. I picked it up and started for the door, but on impulse I paused and looked back at the children. Douglas was in the crib with his blue-and-red-checked blanket, which he kept close at all times, clutched to his chest. Debbie and Donny were huddled in the center of a double bed. Debbie's hair fanned the pillow and fell onto Donny's hand. They were peaceful and defenseless and I felt love for them.

I looked at Gene. He was on his side snoring, his dark hair tousled. He seemed as defenseless as the children against my plan to drink. And I thought, *I love you. I can't do this to you.*

Maybe it was the first moment of honest love I had ever felt for him.

I dropped the wallet on the table.

I took off my coat. And while I hung it, my teeth started to chatter. It had been too close. A dollar and I'd have been in a bar. Deeply frightened, I went to the phone and gave the operator Pat's number.

Be home, be home, I thought.

She was home. And to my review of the last half hour, she said, "God's looking after you."

I couldn't agree, for I wasn't sure that God existed. "It wasn't God; it was lack of money."

"Someday—"

I interrupted. I had almost gotten drunk. I had to get advice. "What should I do?"

"Have you called someone there in A.A.?"

"No."

"Call in the morning. Get yourself started with a new group. And get a sponsor. You're too new to do this alone. And," she added with a pause for emphasis, "pray."

I hung up soon. Pat's advice, even the sound of her voice had reassured me. And suddenly I felt exhilarated. The desire to drink was gone. I felt the power of my will to overcome and decided it would be useless to pray. What could prayer do for me? For I had overcome! I had conquered and I had not gotten drunk!

I pulled off my slacks and sweater and wriggled into my nightgown. I slid into bed beside Gene, leaned over, and kissed his forehead. He did not wake up.

In the morning the bed rocked, waking me. I felt Gene roll from the bed and heard him walk to the bathroom. I remembered the love I had felt last night and I wanted to tell Gene about it. Impatiently, I listened to the water in the shower.

Finally, Gene opened the door. He was wearing a brown long-sleeved shirt and jeans, and his face was flushed, his hair wet.

I sat and touched the mattress. "Come over for a minute."

He came, sat, and took me in his arms. "Good morning, darling," he said.

He put his face in my neck. He was warm and damp and smelled of soap and after-shave. "Last night . . . " That was all I could get out. Somehow my feeling for him had gone as flat as a day-old glass of champagne. I was close to tears. Was it possible to fall out of love with someone this quickly? I doubted it. Rather, it must be that I lacked the ability to sustain love. Maybe I would never be able to love him.

"Last night . . . " he prompted.

"I slept pretty well."

"I did too."

"Good," I said.

He pulled back and glanced at his watch. "We'd better get the kids up. The van's due at nine."

Gene woke Douglas and I woke Debbie and Donny. We dressed, ate, I called A.A. We met the moving van. I unpacked the kitchen cartons and Gene put the bed frames together and unpacked the bathroom cartons. We rushed all day. I did not think about drinking or love. We fell into bed exhausted and immediately slept.

Our ranch house was located on Kosta Drive, which was called "the neighborhood" by the residents.

Every house on Kosta Drive and McCreary Court, an adjoining cul-de-sac, was a seven-room ranch, in floor plan the exact duplicate of ours. For variety, though, some were buff brick, some red brick, some tan brick.

With few exceptions, the residents ranged in age from twenty-five to forty. Gene, thirty, and I, twenty-nine, fit right in. Also, with few exceptions the men were white-collar workers: engineers, junior executives, salesmen, teachers. Most of the men, like Gene, hoped to succeed.

Shortly after moving in, I was invited to neighborhood bridge parties and coffee klatches and the area Welcome Wagon club. In addition I attended Monday and Thursday night A.A. meetings. I told no one in the neighborhood about the A.A. meetings, not even Elsie Saunders, a neighbor who was becoming my closest friend. The problem was, if I told Elsie, she might tell another. Soon everyone would know that I was alcoholic, therefore to be pitied. I abhorred pity. And even worse, they would all be watching and wondering, *Will she make it?* Under that kind of surveillance I would be a nervous wreck.

I wondered if anyone questioned where I went every Monday and Thursday evening. I dreaded someone asking. If he did, where could I tell him I went? What kind of club or group met with the same frequency as A.A.? As far as I knew, none did.

Finally, someone did ask. It was September, seven months

after we had come to Cincinnati. I was having coffee in Elsie Saunders' spotless kitchen. We were trading banter about our families when she gave me an odd look—reluctant, yet at the same time curious. "There's something I'd like to ask you," she said.

"Go ahead."

"I noticed you go out Monday and Thursday nights. Do you belong to some other clubs besides Welcome Wagon?"

The question I had feared was asked, and my heart began to pound. I wanted to give her a lie, but my mind was blank. What could I say? Could I plead a stomachache and leave? Then to my surprise, I found myself saying, "I go to A.A. meetings."

Her eyes widened.

"I'm an alcoholic. I go to the meetings so I won't drink."

At the admission my heart slowed and I found myself telling her about my drinks while I baby-sat, my drinks alone in the family room in Elmhurst, my first A.A. meeting. For me it was a catharsis. And though I noted that Elsie had her eyes fastened on me and was listening so intently that a dust storm could have rolled through her house unnoticed, I didn't note her actual reaction to my story.

I finished with, "I seem to need a couple of meetings a week to keep my sobriety. I guess I always will."

"Oh, Muriel," Elsie said with such great pity that, if I had been standing, my knees would have buckled.

In defense I said, "It can happen to anybody. Nobody's immune from alcoholism."

"What an awful experience."

I felt nauseated. "It wasn't so awful."

"What can I do to help?"

"Nothing. I'm all right. I'm doing fine. I go to A.A. and I try to live one day at a time."

In her eyes was fierce determination to help. "There must be something."

"Really, nothing."

"If you ever feel like you need to talk, please—"

"Don't tell anybody about this," I interrupted.

"I won't tell a soul."

With that promise, I left.

I watched the actions and the eyes of the women in the

neighborhood. But I was treated as I had always been treated. Their eyes did not question. Elsie, it seemed, had not told a soul. She remained filled with concern and pity, and though a year younger than I, she became a mother to me. Daily, or more frequently, she phoned and asked if everything were all right, or if I would come for coffee, or if I would go shopping. She kept her eyes on me. Oddly, her watching went a long way toward keeping me sober; I would prove I was just fine.

Then on a warm night in late October, Gene and I sat on our patio. Gene was giving me his opinion of Elsie Saunders. "She's kind. She's a caring person."

"She's intrusive," I countered. "I don't like that."

"Then break off the relationship."

"I can't."

"Why?"

"I like her."

"Brother!"

"Nothing's all black or all white."

"Maybe not."

Gene stretched out his legs, and we looked out into the cemetery. After a while I said, "About the A.A. meeting Thursday night."

"I don't want to go."

His usual response. Everytime I invited him to the monthly open meeting (open to family and friends), he refused. But I was determined to bring him, for I had heard in A.A. that the alcoholic's drinking often made the spouse emotionally ill. Though I saw no sign of emotional disturbance in Gene, and he insisted he had none, I thought he should attend A.A. and find out for sure if he were all right.

"Gene, just once. Then I'll never ask again."

"I told you, I'm not mentally ill. I'm not interested in going. There's nothing wrong with me."

"It could be hidden. You could be mentally strained without knowing it."

"It's not hidden. A person knows if he's all right or not."

"Please go, just once."

"No."

"Please, for me."

"All right. Just once. Just to get it over with."

At the meeting, from the moment we walked into the room

and took our seats to the moment we left, Gene's mouth was drawn tight in discomfort. He didn't laugh when the speaker cracked jokes, and after the meeting, over coffee and cake, he said little to my A.A. friends. But as we left the room, his expression relaxed.

In the car I said, "You didn't like it, did you?"

"No. Don't quiz me on this, Muriel. I'm just not comfortable at an A.A. meeting. I think A.A.'s great for you, but it's for you, not me. I'm a person who can take care of himself." He added gently, "Do you understand?"

"Yes, I understand. You're a private person."

"That's not it. I'm a *strong* person. I don't let others get the best of me. I carry on with what I've got to do despite them."

"Is that why you never left when I drank?"

"Probably."

"I won't invite you to a meeting again."

CHAPTER XII

I was serving spaghetti. It was March, almost spring, five months after the A.A. open meeting. I put the plates on the table and poured milk for the children, coffee for Gene and me. With a dispirited look, Douglas picked up his fork, twirled the noodles into a hill, untwirled them, twirled them up again. "Stop playing with your food and eat," Gene said.

Douglas took a small bite and set down his fork. "I don't feel so good," he said.

"Where?" I asked.

"No place."

I put my hand on his forehead. It was dry and hot, and his skin was flushed, his eyes dull. "I'd better get him to bed," I said.

In his bedroom while I put on his pajamas, he was docile and limp as a doll. I took his temperature: 102 degrees. I gave him an aspirin and pulled the covers to his chin. Immediately, he slept.

Back in the kitchen I said to Gene, "I think he's got the flu."

"Probably," Gene said.

"You'll watch him closely tonight."

"Of course."

In a couple of hours I would be leaving to play bridge at Paula Dawes'. A few months ago Paula and her husband, Jim, had moved onto Kosta Drive. Already they were quite popular, and were invited to every party in the neighborhood. Everyone, including me, was attracted to Paula. She had a magnetic personality and was breath-catchingly beautiful. In addition she was smart, a Phi Beta Kappa with a degree in biology. And beyond all that she would be well-off soon, for Jim, though only thirty-two, was a district sales manager and was slated, according to Paula, for a top job in his company.

Paula had everything. But even though I was attracted to her, I didn't like her. In her presence I felt ugly and inferior—and jealous.

At Paula's I started out at table two, which was beside a tier of bookshelves. Somehow three tables of bridge did not jam up Paula's living room and dining room the way they would have mine. In some mysterious way everything worked out for Paula, it seemed, far better than anything could work out for me.

My partner was Grace Kiefer, my opponents, Paula Dawes and Marion Neel. While Grace shuffled the spare deck, I dealt. Everyone picked up her cards, sorted them into suits, and continued talking about husbands, whom each had been discussing the last five minutes. Not listening, I studied my hand.

As the hand was quite good, I wanted to get on with the game. "Two no-trump," I said.

They kept on talking.

"Two no-trump," I said again.

No response.

"It's your bid," I said to Paula, but she didn't hear me. Her full attention was given to Grace who was saying, "I'm fed up with Gordy. With him it's nothing but golf and bowling."

"With Jim it's long hours," said Paula. She tossed her head back, throwing her waves of hair out from her shoulders.

"I'd rather have Jim's hours than Gordy's sports," said Grace. "We never talk."

"Two no-trump," I said, but again got no response.

I did not enter the conversation, because I could add nothing. Gene wasn't addicted to golf and bowling, he didn't keep long hours, he didn't ignore me. He was a superior husband. He loved me. But I didn't love him. And if I told that fact to these women, they would think it a fascinating dichotomy and would give me reams of advice on how to love.

But the answer lay not in advice, I thought, *but in my emotions.* Then I felt as if I were having a moment of insight, for I saw that I kept my thoughts so steadily on myself that there wasn't an opening available for Gene. If I could discover how to send some of my thoughts toward him, then my emotions would change and I would feel love for him. But how did I go about doing that?

Paula said, "Your bid, Muriel." I heard her, but I was slow in getting my mind back to my bridge hand and didn't answer.

"Wake up," Paula said.

"Sorry."

"Where was your mind?"

"On Gene, I guess."

"What about him?"

"He's a pretty good husband."

"Come on. Nobody's perfect."

"I guess not." I quickly came up with a fault. "He swears a lot."

"Swearing's a mark of a limited vocabulary," Paula replied. "A person can't come up with an appropriate word and he swears for emphasis. I've heard Gene. He does swear too much."

"I know."

"Your bid," said Grace.

"Two no-trump," I said. Grace responded three no-trump and I made four. We played till after midnight.

When I came home I passed our living room window, and saw Gene sitting on the couch with Douglas in his arms. I flung open the door, went to them, and brushed Douglas' hair with my hand. "He's gotten sicker, hasn't he?" I asked.

"Yes. Quite a bit."

Douglas' breathing was shallow and labored and his face was still flushed. He bent his head into Gene's shoulder and coughed. "When did he start that gasping and coughing?" I asked.

"I don't know. While I was sleeping, I guess. About a half hour ago his coughing woke me."

I saw the thermometer on the coffee table. "You took his temperature?"

"It's a hundred and three."

Because I had been reading medical articles in magazines and newspapers for years, I put together the difficult breathing, coughing, high fever and decided that Douglas probably had pneumonia. I said, "There's a good chance he's got pneumonia. I think we should call Dr. Rose."

Douglas did have pneumonia, and Dr. Rose put him on an antibiotic and ordered him to bed. A week and a half later, Douglas was up and eating well, apparently recovered. But the recovery was short-lived; within a few days his temperature shot up, his breathing became labored, he coughed. The pneumonia was back. Douglas was hospitalized and tested, for the successive bouts of pneumonia could mean that he had aspirated a small object, like a peanut. To our relief, the tests were negative. As before, Douglas responded to rest and antibiotics. He was discharged in a week.

The day he came home, he weighed 29 pounds, a scanty weight for a 3 1/2-year-old. His arms and legs were like broomsticks, his face pale, his freckles in relief, like coffee splashes against a bleached sheet. His appearance troubled me. In an attempt to put weight on him, I fixed his favorite foods. His face did fill out a little, and I thought he was heading toward good health. But several days after he came home from the hospital, he was sick again.

This time it was not pneumonia, but the flu. For two days Douglas ate only gelatin and crackers and drank only water. His weight dropped to 28 pounds. Frightening thoughts came to me. Was he in a cycle of sickness? Would the flu be followed by a third bout of pneumonia? Would his weight continue to plunge until he died?

I tried to express my fear to Gene. "Do you think Douglas could. . . ?" I couldn't finish the sentence.

"Could?"

"Do you think he'll get better?"

"I think so," Gene said. But his eyes clouded and I suspected he was as worried as I.

The third morning of Douglas' flu, I carried his breakfast to his room. In a listless way, he poked at the crackers, took a few bites of gelatin, a few sips of orange juice. In an attempt to perk him up, I brought him to my bed and gave him two small puzzles to piece together, one of a rabbit, one of a sailboat. He went right to work, and I left to clean the hall bathroom. I sprinkled the tub with cleanser and began scrubbing, but while I was still working the cleanser, Douglas called, "Mommy. Come here, Mommy."

I dropped my rag and hurried to him. I thought he had become hungry and wanted the tray I had left in his room. "Are you hungry, darling?" I said.

"No."

"Then what is it?"

"Am I going to grow up?"

His eyes were round and intense. Stunned, I stared at him for long moments, sure now that his illnesses would end in death. And Douglas knew it. Some supernatural perception had given him the knowledge. Maybe all people at the point of death possessed such perception.

In an even voice, I said, "Of course, you'll grow up. Someday you'll be a dad just like your own dad."

The thought that Douglas might die made me feel almost hysterical and I threw myself into cleaning the bathroom. *I'm just overreacting*, I kept telling myself.

A while later Douglas called. Certain he had more questions about growing up, I went to him with a sinking feeling.

His puzzle of a rabbit eating a carrot was finished and was lying beside his leg. The puzzle of a sailboat was complete except for a piece of the sail, which he held in his hand.

"Good job," I said. "Are you going to put it in?"

Oddly, he dropped the piece on his lap and leaned forward. "A lady was here. She looked like a mommy."

"A mommy? What do you mean?"

"She had brown hair and a blue dress. She said something."

"What?"

"She said, 'Don't worry, you'll get better.' "

Bewildered, I glanced at the television set just beyond the foot of the bed. It was off, but had Douglas snapped it on?

"Did you see the mommy on television?"

"No."

"What were you doing when she came?"

"Fixing my puzzle."

"Where did she come from?"

"I don't know. She was saying my name and she was here."

"How did she leave?"

"In the air."

On another day in another moment, I might have decided that Douglas was playing make-believe. But at this moment I took in the color that was coming on his pale face and the animation with which he spoke. A vigor that had not been with him earlier was with him now; I believed his story.

I remembered that Elsie Saunders believed in angels. And somehow my spirit and thoughts must have been touched by God, for I found myself thinking: *The woman was an angel, sent by God.* I felt the truth of it. And I felt that Douglas would get well.

Suddenly the full impact of what I was thinking hit me. I was believing in the existence of God. I started to cry, for as far back as I could remember, I had wanted to believe in Him.

I hugged Douglas and said, "The mommy was an angel. God sent her."

"Is God a friend?"

"Yes. He's the One who made angels. He lives in heaven and—"

All excited, Douglas interrupted. "Heaven's where Petey went." Petey, a neighbor's cat, had died last month. The neighbor had told Douglas that Petey had gone to heaven.

"Yes," I said.

"I'm not sick like Petey was."

"No, you're not."

The day after Douglas saw the angel, he was out of bed. "You can sit quietly, but don't run," I warned. With an obvious effort, he sat, but it was as if he were a compressed spring.

The following day he dashed through the house, rolled across the carpet, and crawled after his truck. "Don't be so wild," I said, delighted with his wildness.

That night after I put the children in bed, I found Gene in the garage waxing the Volkswagen. I sat on a cardboard box.

"You're welcome to help," he said.

"I don't feel like it. I came out to talk about something."

I told him about the woman that Douglas had seen. "I think it was an angel," I said.

"It was nothing."

"It was, too, something. I could tell by his face."

Gene set his rag on the hood and leaned against the fender. "More likely the episode happened in his imagination. He had a fever and he became delirious and thought he saw a woman."

"He saw a woman—an angel, and because of it I believe in God. I'd like to be a more religious person. I'd like to start going to church. I'm planning to take the kids. I hope you'll want to come, too."

"I'd like to."

"I expected some resistance. I thought you got sick of church when you were a kid."

"People change."

"Then you believe in God?"

"No," he said and picked up his rag. "It's that I think it's time our kids learned some sound Christian values. I think I should set the example. If they see me in church, they'll know I stand for right principles."

CHAPTER XIII

At the sprawling church with the large congregation that we had chosen to attend, the minister was praying with authority and I felt close to God. I cried, as I always did when this happened. It was late May, several weeks after the angel had come. Douglas had gained three pounds and was inquisitive, cheerful, energetic. I had been trying to take the third step of the Twelve Steps: "Made a decision to turn our will and our lives over to the care of God *as we understood Him*."

I loved these times of prayer here, when I could touch God and He would touch me. Unfortunately, my spirit would fall flat when the minister started into one of his usual boring, three-part sermons on self-improvement. And even worse, my spirit couldn't reach up to God during the week because I didn't know how to pray with the authority of the minister. And I would feel far from God as if my life were not in His care. The only time I felt a close association was in prayer in church. *If only I could pray as the minister prayed*, I thought.

But now the prayer was finished and the sermon began. It was awful and I didn't listen.

Toward the end of the week I was thinking about the prayer at church. I wondered if the minister would teach me to pray effectively. *Of course, he would,* I thought.

Excited at the prospect, I phoned the church. The minister was out for the day, but the assistant minister, the Reverend Art Benson, agreed to stop by and discuss prayer.

By late morning Mr. Benson was seated at the kitchen table. He was about thirty and reed-thin with large blue eyes that held a reserved and reluctant look. I poured him a cup of coffee and put a plate of fresh cookies on the table. "Please help yourself. I just baked them."

"Thanks." He took one, bit off half, and popped the second half into his mouth. "They're delicious," he said. His two bites surprised me. He seemed like a person who would nibble around the edges and work in to the middle.

"How long have you lived here?" he asked.

"Almost sixteen months."

"Where does your husband work?"

I told him, and with more such questions the visit inched along, until finally I broke in with, "When I called, I asked if we could talk about prayer."

"Of course."

"I want to learn how to pray effectively. I want to grow close to God."

"Is there some problem in your life for which you need prayer? In other words, is there a special reason you want to, as you so nicely said, 'grow close to God'?"

"It's nothing special. It's everything."

"Everything?"

Suddenly a great sadness flooded me. I blurted out, "It's the way my life's been." I looked into the Reverend Benson's eyes and found myself telling him about my alcoholism, my sobriety, the angel. While I spoke, he kept his eyes from me and on his coffee cup and the table. I found the lack of eye contact disconcerting. *I must be upsetting him*, I thought. *I shouldn't be laying my past before this uneasy, shy man. I should stop—now.* But I felt compelled to finish, because it was, as it had been at Elsie Saunders', a catharsis. At the end I concluded with, "I'm sorry. I might've said more than I should."

He now looked at me, and I understood why he had been watching his cup and the table. His eyes were misty. He was close to tears, but he was holding them back. "You didn't," he said.

"You can see I need to learn to pray."

"We all do."

"I feel empty all the time. I feel like there's nothing inside me. I need God to be near."

"He will be. He wants to be."

"I hope so."

The Reverend Benson then told me that the next week, for three days, there would be a prayer seminar at a downtown church. He would be going. "Would you like to come along?" he asked. "This might be just the kind of experience you're looking for."

"I think I'd like it."

The prayer seminar was held in the basement of the downtown church. Along with the Reverend Benson, one woman from our church, and me, there were about sixty people from the fifty-plus area churches within the denomination. "Why so few?" I asked Mr. Benson, while we waited for the meeting to begin. "You'd think there'd be hundreds."

"Lack of interest."

"But why the lack?" My question, though, remained unanswered, for the chairman was coming to the front of the room. He welcomed us to the seminar, prayed we would have an inspiring experience, then split us into small discussion groups.

"I thought this would be a lecture," I said to Mr. Benson. "I can't discuss prayer in a group. I came to learn."

"Just listen," he said. "You'll be fine." He stood and picked up his folding chair and headed for his group.

I took my chair and went to my group. There were four of us: a woman close to my age, who glanced shyly at me as I put down my chair; a short, round woman of about fifty; a man in his thirties with a black mustache that swept up thickly toward his ears.

The man said, "I'm your discussion leader. It looks like we're all here."

After we exchanged names, churches, and occupations, our leader said, "I hope we can share our feelings about prayer without being self-conscious. I myself have been praying now for over thirty years. My mother taught me to take my problems to God." He then explained that in order to have a successful prayer life, a person must get himself into a relaxed setting and unwind.

Earlier, so that I could take notes, I had put a small spiral notebook into my purse. I now took it out and wrote, "Relax your mind before praying."

The older woman glanced around our small circle and said, "I find I've got to have a definite time and spot. I always pray at seven in the morning in my brown chair."

The leader nodded, and I wrote, "Establish a time and spot for prayer."

"But I can't count on a regular time," said the younger woman in a voice so quiet that I strained to hear. "I've got a baby, and in the morning after I feed him, I feed my little girl and my husband. And then I've got the dishes, and . . . " Her words faded out.

The older woman said, "It doesn't have to be in the morning, dear. The important thing's to find a time and stick to it."

"I'll try," said the younger woman.

I paused with my pencil poised above the notebook. I was becoming impatient with the superficiality of the discussion and wondered if I should note that comment. I did. "Prayer hour can be any hour."

"I like to pray on my knees," said the leader. "The position increases my supplicatory attitude."

I made my one comment of the discussion. "Do you feel closer to God on your knees? Do you feel as if He's with you?"

"Sometimes that's the case," he said. And that was all he said.

He and the others then went on to discussing prayer in church, prayer for those in hospitals, prayer while occupied with daily matters. I dropped my notebook in my purse, crossed my arms over my chest, and quit listening. I disliked the seminar and these narrow people who could not leave the mechanics of prayer and go on to reach God. At A.A. meetings we got to the heart of the subject under discussion. At A.A. meetings I learned something. These people were too churchy, too full of prayer rules, too protected, viewing the world from their church pews. Thank heavens, I'd lived in the world. Thank heavens, I didn't pray at eight in the morning on my knees.

Later, as we left, Mr. Benson asked, "How did it go?"

His eyes were so kind, so hoping that I had liked it, that I couldn't tell him how awful it had been. "It was fine," I said.

"You'll be coming tomorrow?" he asked.

"I can't."

"The next night?"

"I wish I could, but I'm busy all week."

"I'm sorry."

"I'm sorry, too."

At home I found Gene in bed reading the newspaper, and I said to him, "The meeting was a catastrophe." While I sat on the edge of the bed, Gene gave me a startled look, for my voice was harsh. "I hated it," I continued. "It was a how-to approach to prayer. All church people are bound up. They can't see the forest for the trees. They can't see God for the prayer. The A.A.'s aren't bound up like that."

"A.A.'s are in a different situation. They're fighting for their lives. If they aren't open and honest, they'll get drunk. The people at your seminar haven't got a compelling reason to spill out their guts."

"I wasn't expecting them to spill out their guts. I was just expecting a discussion of prayer power and God."

"That's a very personal subject."

"It is not."

I couldn't see Gene's point, and in a few days I had extrapolated my dislike of prayer seminars into a dislike of my church. I would not return.

As it turned out, we all stopped going to church. My negative attitude affected Gene and he lost his interest in church. He could, he said, teach the children Christian values just as well as the church could. But the children missed Sunday school and often asked us to take them. I would tell them, "Maybe someday."

One Sunday morning as Gene and I lay in bed late, I said, "We should get up and drop the kids off at Sunday school. My parents used to drop off my sisters and me."

He nodded and yawned and was soon sleeping again. I slept too.

Somehow we always managed to stay up so late playing bridge on Saturday night that we couldn't get up and drive the children to Sunday school.

For the most part, I stopped praying. For God didn't respond to my prayers with direct answers that I could understand, or with a presence that I could feel. Praying, it seemed, was walking on nothing toward God.

I still kept my belief in God, but I thought less and less about Him. For some reason perhaps God expected certain people, like me, to handle most of their own affairs.

One day the Reverend Mr. Benson telephoned, "We've missed you. Is everything all right?" he asked.

Not wanting to hurt him, I lied. "We're just taking a short break. Everything's fine. We're busy, but we'll be back."

Several days after his call, I read an article about a church whose membership included atheists, agnostics, and a few who believed in God, very few. The membership believed that truth was ever-changing and they searched to know it. They believed in the beauty of the human intellect and they admired it. I imagined the absorbing, stimulating, intellectual services the church would have.

I loved what I imagined and that evening on the deck I told Gene about the church.

"I really think we should go," I said. "I'm sure it's our kind of church."

"Where is it?"

"There's one three miles away."

"It sounds good," he said.

"Then let's go."

On Sunday we went. After bringing the children to their Sunday school rooms, we were seated in a stark, white room with folding chairs instead of pews, a lectern on the hardwood floor instead of a raised altar, and clear glass windows instead of stained glass. On the wall behind the lectern was a ceiling-to-floor mural. There was no cross. Oddly, I wished there were.

The service opened with a reading from Shakespeare, followed by an Italian aria, then a speaker. Since the church did not have a minister, either members or invited guests gave the sermon, more appropriately titled a lecture. Today's speaker was a rabbi who compared Reform Judaism, Orthodox Judaism, and Christianity. Throughout the comparison, the rabbi interjected his own philosophy of atheism. I found his lecture weighty, wordy and offensive. Several times my attention wandered. Gene, though, obviously was following him closely.

The service was followed by a coffee hour. We stayed and talked to several couples. I found them all intelligent, articulate, friendly. I liked them, but Gene especially seemed to like them. Although usually quiet with strangers, he was verbal, enthusiastically discussing the lecture, freely sharing his agnostic philosophy.

While driving home, I said to Gene, "I'm not that hot on

going back. The atheism makes me uncomfortable."

"Let's give the church a chance, gal."

"I don't like it," said Debbie. "It's boring."

"It's not like Sunday school," said Douglas.

"What did you talk about?" I asked.

"How trees make bugs so we can have woodpeckers in the forest," said Douglas.

"You mean how bugs live in trees," I said. "Trees don't make bugs."

"I like it that they teach the kids about nature," said Gene.

"You seem to like everything about the place. You really do want to go back, don't you?"

"Yes. I don't think you should be so quick to judge it."

He was right. And beyond that I felt a responsibility to try because I had introduced Gene to the church. "Okay, let's give it a chance."

So we continued to attend the church. At no time was there prayer, at no time a hymn which honored or even mentioned God. Every speaker was either an atheist or an agnostic. I missed God and prayer. On our fourth Sunday, instead of a speaker, we had a panel of three white couples who had recently moved into black neighborhoods. The discussion was a welcome break from the atheistic speakers, and I listened with interest.

After the service we discussed racial prejudice with Kate and Walt Laugel, a highly educated couple about our age; he had a Ph.D. in chemistry, she a Ph.D. in physics.

Gene asked, "Do you think whites will ever want to live with blacks?"

"Well, as you see, some do. But in general most people's attitudes need to undergo a vast adjustment," said Walt.

"It'll take a lot of prayer," I said, forgetting that few in the church believed in prayer. Then remembering, I said, "You're right. People need to work on their attitudes."

Ignoring my adjustment, Walt said, "Interesting idea. Can our words or thoughts, or as you say, prayers, change our basic attitudes? I don't know." He began speaking rapidly, as if rushing to keep up with his thoughts. "But the mind's vastly underrated. I've read that a patient who trusts his medicine will improve faster than one who doesn't. It makes me wonder if belief triggers a chemical reaction in the brain that produces a result coincident with the belief." Walt touched Kate's arm.

"Would you agree?"

"Possibly," Kate said. "But if I extend your theory, then I must conclude that belief can produce anything, even God."

"Exactly," Walt said. He paused, then added, "We have God, then, an erroneous conception produced by an erroneous belief. And we have prayer, as Muriel called it, or thought projection, as I would say, as the vehicle of belief that produces the illusion of God."

His conclusion amazed me. How could he be right? God was not a chemical reaction to thought projection; God was God.

I looked at Gene. His eyes were graying, as they did when he was troubled. He said, "Your theory completely axes the possibility that God might exist. I don't think we can go that far."

I felt my mouth open in surprise. I would have expected Gene to jump in and expand on Walt's theory.

"You don't believe that belief can produce a concept?" Walt replied.

"Of course, I do. But what I'm saying is that God may be an actuality."

A few minutes later we left the Laugels, found the children, and started down the sidewalk toward the car. The sun was burning down and I perspired. But after that cold, stark church, the heat felt good. "It's good to be outside," I said. "I'm sick of this church."

"I am too."

"Because of what Walt said?"

"Partly."

"Is it partly because of the atheism?"

"Don't take this too far, Muriel. I didn't tell Walt I believed in God. I just said He might exist. I'm not a religious person. I don't pray. I don't spend my time thinking about God."

"I don't that much either."

"You do more than I do."

"When I look at things like the petunias and the trees, I think it's easier to be close to God outside then inside a church."

"I can't say that because I don't have your feelings about God."

We were at the car. We got in and Gene backed up and

started toward the road.

"I think I'd rather go walking than go to church," I said.

"Fine."

"You don't care if we don't go back?"

"Not at all."

CHAPTER XIV

In the early fall, several weeks after we stopped going to churches, I was sitting on the couch in the living room hating Paula Dawes. It still bothered me greatly that last spring she had run against me for the presidency of Welcome Wagon and had won. And it bothered me that she was popular, smart and beautiful. But today I had really gotten upset when I had found out that she and her husband were invited to the Petersons' dinner party and Gene and I were not.

It was hard to believe that I was once even slightly attracted to that woman.

If only I were beautiful and popular like Paula.

I was so upset that I felt like going to the garage and searching through the cardboard cartons for the liquor bottles. To guard against moments like this, shortly after we moved in, I asked Gene to hide the liquor in the garage. We kept the liquor on hand to serve to friends. My theory in hiding the bottles was that by the time I found them, I would have second thoughts about drinking. Also, I believed that liquor out of sight was liquor out of mind. To date I had not gotten to the point where I searched through the cartons. But several times in these last months, I'd fought through some rough hours— like now. These times were usually brought on by jealousy or anger or some one of my many character defects. I wanted to eliminate the defects, because I had learned in A.A. that giving them rein might cause me to drink. It was quite possible that I could be wildly jealous, hate myself, then drink in hope that I would like myself and be happy.

Now, rather than go to the garage, I went to the backyard where Gene was mowing the grass. I held up my hand, and he cut the engine. "What do you think of Paula Dawes?" I asked.

"She's intelligent—she's interesting to talk to."

"Is she prettier than I?"

"I wouldn't say that. She has different looks than you, but she's very pretty."

"I don't like her. She's a surface person and a gossip."

"I've never heard her gossip."

"I have. She gossips a lot."

"Why are you so against her?"

"I just don't care for her type," I said, and left.

All evening I fought going to the garage. I didn't go, but later I fell into bed, drained.

Though she did an excellent job, of course, I hated watching Paula chair the meeting. And a few days later I said to Gene, "I might quit Welcome Wagon."

"Why?"

Not about to tell him of my jealousy for Paula, I said, "I'm getting tired of it. I'm not a newcomer anymore."

"I thought you went because you had friends there."

"I do."

"Then why quit?"

"I don't know. I guess I won't."

I stayed. And it became easier to sit through the Welcome Wagon meetings, but I never exactly liked the experience.

Then not many months later, our lease on Kosta Drive expired and we bought a small ranch-style home on Fountainbleau Terrace, three miles from the "neighborhood." As on Kosta Drive, our new ranch house was on a quarter acre and had seven rooms, two baths, no basement. But there the similarity ended. On Fountainbleau we bordered a forest, not a cemetery. Here there would be no funerals, thank heavens. Here I wouldn't have to see Paula Dawes so often. Thank heavens.

In the move we left that Welcome Wagon district. Though I was invited to stay, I made friends in my new area and soon stopped going to the meetings. Time and little contact did take the edge from my jealousy, but the depth it had taken scared me. *I must work at improving my character*, I thought. Taking my lead from steps 4-7 of the A.A. program, I made a list of my defects, with jealousy heading the list. In my case, though, I, not God, would be removing the defects. For I didn't think God would or could remove them.

So I would strive to improve and become a better person. Then I would stay sober and someday be happy. As yet, in my sobriety I had experienced little happiness or serenity.

But before I got on very far with improving myself, I tripped over two women: Bonnie and Carla.

The first time I saw Bonnie was at my Tuesday night A.A. meeting, held in the corner room of a church. She was swaying across the room behind Diane, a longtime member of the group. Bonnie was heavy, about 170 pounds, and it seemed that at any moment she would tip over and crash. But she made it to my table, pulled out a chair across from mine, and sat. "Hi ya," she said with a lopsided grin.

"Hi," I said.

"Diane brought me," she said.

"I know."

"I'm new. I quit drinking last night."

Impossible, I thought. She was obviously drunk. She was uncoordinated, her eyes watered, her face was puffed, her breath smelled like gales of gin.

"Last night?" I said.

"Yes." Bonnie gave a sigh and added, "Diane says the first day's the worst." Craning her neck, she squinted at me, as if I were not before her, but twenty feet away. "Are you new, too?"

"No, I've been sober for over two years."

Tuesday after Tuesday Bonnie came to the meeting and weaved across the room behind Diane. Smiling, sighing, and smelling like a distillery, she would fall into a chair and tell us that she was sober and doing just fine.

Her lying drove me nuts. *Be patient, be loving*, I thought, remembering my list of defects. But I felt frustration and dislike, not patience and love.

Then one Tuesday night, shortly before the meeting began, I was chatting with the women at my table, but keeping my eyes on the door. Any minute Bonnie would reel in. *I hate liars*, I thought, forgetting that I often had and still did, lie.

And there she was, barely able to walk, swinging in behind Diane. She plunked into a chair, a perfect shot.

"Hi ya," she said. She grinned and waved her arm, including everyone at the table.

"Hi," I said. Knowing her answer would boil me, I asked, "How's it going?"

"Terrible. The refrigerator broke and my son ran into a parked car." She sighed and opened her purse and looked in. "But at least I've got my sobriety."

"You do?" I said, feeling anger flare. "Really?"

"Nine weeks now." She lifted her head and blinked earnestly.

That did it. I exploded. "You're not sober, you're drunk!"

"I'm sober." She clenched her lower lip with her teeth, an abortive attempt at a pout. Although she was pathetic, I felt no sympathy. I noted, though, that the five women at my table were watching Bonnie with great concern.

Bonnie released her lip and gave me a sorrowful gaze, like that of a homeless rabbit. But in my anger, I continued, "You're not sober. We don't come here to learn to drink. We don't come to the meetings plastered, and we don't lie."

With tears rolling down her cheeks, she said, "I'm very sober. I'm perfectly all right."

She picked up her purse, stumbled from her chair, and tottered from the room, as if fighting through a squall. The five women at my table jumped up and followed her, leaving me alone. Obviously, they thought my outburst cruel. And it was.

Ashamed, I followed the group down the hall and into the rest room. There Bonnie hung over the sink and the five women huddled around her. Bonnie raised up and pointed at me and said. "She—she—told me I was drunk and I'm not. She—acted like I'm a liar." Diane reached for Bonnie, and Bonnie laid her head on Diane's shoulder and sobbed. "She—she—said I lied."

"That's okay, that's okay," Diane said, patting Bonnie's back. "Muriel didn't mean to hurt you."

"I didn't," I said. "I'm sorry."

Raising her eyes to me, but keeping her chin on Diane's shoulder, Bonnie said, "You called me a liar."

123

"I know, but I'm sorry. I didn't mean to."

"You hurt me."

"I know, I know. I'm sorry."

Bonnie's tears darkened Diane's blouse. She was obviously too upset to listen. I hugged my arms in close and knew I was too upset to continue apologizing. Without another word I left.

I thought, *I've really messed up. How could I have blown up at a person as pathetic as Bonnie? Yet how can she sober up if she can't admit she's drunk? I shouldn't have said what I did, in the way that I did, but she's got to face herself sometime.*

Later at home in bed, I tried to read a novel but couldn't. I laid it on the bedside table and moved close to Gene. I laid my head on his shoulder in somewhat the same way Bonnie had put her head on Diane's shoulder. Still feeling awful, I needed to touch someone who cared about me. I related the incident with Bonnie. "The women all stayed with her," I said in conclusion. "They didn't see my side at all."

"They had a point," he said. "You shouldn't have confronted her like that. At Procter and Gamble we wouldn't do it that way."

"What would you do?"

"We talk to a person. We find out what the problem is, then deal with it."

"But anybody could see she was drunk."

"It doesn't matter. We don't accuse like that."

"Those women think I'm hard as nails."

"You're not hard." Gene turned, wrapped his arms around me, and kissed me. "I love you."

That brought tears and I said, "I'm glad you do."

The next Tuesday, Bonnie strode into the A.A. meeting behind Diane with her head high and her walk as straight as an arrow. She smoothly pulled out the chair diagonally from me and neatly sat down. She then set her purse on the floor and said "Hi ya" to everyone at the table. Her glance around the table as she greeted us included me.

Even from my distance, I smelled the mint on her breath as she spoke.

Bonnie was finally sober.

Neither she nor I mentioned last week.

At home while Gene heated the coffeepot, I told him about Bonnie's sobriety. "It turned out your blast helped her," he said.

"Partly. But that's not the only reason she got sober."

"No, but I'm sure it contributed."

"I guess it did."

"Then why the unhappy expression?"

"Because I don't like the way I helped her. I wish I'd done it the P & G way. She obviously doesn't like me. She was polite and formal and she never said anything about last week."

"Did you?"

"No."

"Well, maybe she thinks *you* don't like her. After all, you're the one that read her out."

"But she knows I'm sorry."

"Maybe she thought you were saying that to be polite."

"I don't think so," I said.

Gene poured coffee and we dropped the subject of Bonnie.

My emotions on the situation were askew. I wanted her to like me because I liked everyone to like me. I needed the esteem that others gave me. Yet I didn't really like her. But I was pleased she was sober. Yet I was upset that my anger had revealed one of my character defects.

So I should re-apologize and tell her I was happy that she was sober, but I held back for the next several Tuesdays.

Then one Tuesday after the meeting I was saying to the women, "I really did something I shouldn't have last night. I screamed at Donny because he didn't understand my explanation of fractions. I just stood there and yelled at him. I've got to be more patient."

"You do," said Bonnie. It was her first direct comment to me and I knew she was referring to that night.

"I'm going to be." I suspected she knew I was referring to the same night. "But sometimes a little temper can catch someone's attention. Maybe Donny hasn't been listening to his teacher and that's why he doesn't understand fractions."

"Probably."

It was a truce.

But it still upset me that I had blown up at her. I wanted to be a loving person. Like Gene. I thought of how he loved me despite my imperfections. If I really wanted to put my character defects behind me, I'd reach to have that kind of love for others.

Just as I came to that insight, I backed off and thought, *I was doing the best I could. I have to stop dwelling on every nit-picking defect in my character. If I keep on like this, I'll start hating myself and I'll drink.*

From then on Bonnie and I were easier with each other, but we didn't become friends. I worked on my character defects, the simpler ones, such as anger, envy, pride, etc. Then several months into Bonnie's sobriety, I met Carla, and I stumbled again.

She phoned one morning. "You don't know me," she said, "but I'm Carla and I live on Mockingbird Lane. A.A. headquarters gave me your number because they said you live nearby. I just moved here." Her words slurred and faltered, and I pressed the receiver to my ear. I thought she was drunk.

"Are you all right?" I asked.

"I'm fine. I slur because I had a stroke two years ago." She explained that the same stroke had partially paralyzed her right side, and even though months of therapy brought great improvement, she still walked with a pronounced limp. She said that nobody in the world had her measure of rotten luck. Almost immediately after the stroke her husband, a successful attorney, had died, leaving her to raise their four children (ages 5-19). Then recently dwindling finances had forced her to sell her elegant colonial with great round pillars and buy the small ranch house with a musty basement on Mockingbird Lane. "I had to sell half my furniture," she said. "You can't know what a terrible move down this is." She began a long discourse of her troubles.

I interrupted. "You said A.A. gave you my number?"

"Yes," she said with an edge of impatience.

"Then you've got a drinking problem?"

"I do."

"Would you like to tell me about it?"

"Not over the phone. I don't know you."

"You can trust me. I'm an alcoholic. I've been through everything you've been through."

"Not on the phone."

Her strange reluctance to discuss her drinking problem

must stem from her stroke and her grief, I thought. "Then would you like to go to an A.A. meeting?" I said. "I could pick you up. You could meet me and then maybe we could talk."

"Fine," she said, and I arranged to pick her up for my Friday morning discussion meeting.

When I arrived at her house on Friday, Carla hobbled down the hall without a cane, but with such effort that it seemed as though she were about to stumble. Instinctively, I held out my hand, then dropped it, not wanting to offend her with, perhaps, unwanted help. *Poor woman,* I thought. The right side of her body drooped, with the arm extending limply from her shoulder and rotating inwardly. The right side of her face sagged. Her eyes watered. Blond hair straggled from black roots. She looked down-and-out, as if she belonged in a two-room flat in a shabby tenement.

She said, "You're Muriel?"

"I am."

She came to me, hooked her arm in mine, and dragged along beside me to the car.

En route, she was as talkative as she had been on the phone. "I can't handle any of the children," she said. "You don't know how hard it is." She sighed. "Things would be different if Matt were still here. He had a heart attack two years ago."

"Yes, I remember," I said. Yesterday during the phone call, she had told me in detail about Matt's heart attack and death in the kitchen.

"It's like yesterday," she said. "He went to bed with *The Wall Street Journal,* just like he always did. Then he . . . " And she continued with her sad story.

Although I thought it probably eased her grief to talk about Matt's death, I felt we must move on from that to her drinking. "It must've been a terrible shock," I said, then quickly added, "Can you tell me why you called A.A.?"

"I'm drinking too much."

"For long?"

"No. I hardly drank a drop when Matt was here."

She went back to the story of the heart attack, Matt's death, then went on to the autopsy and funeral, until the meeting began.

During the meeting she was quiet and seemed to listen attentively.

While driving home, I said, "Did you like the meeting?"

"Yes, very much."

"Carla, I think we should talk about the reason you need A.A.—your drinking."

"Of course, that's just recent," she said and veered off into a discussion of Matt's will, which left her a fair amount of money. "But I've got to watch my pennies," she said. "I never had to before. I just don't have the money I used to have."

I gave up and listened to an account of her household expenses. Though I pitied her and wanted to like her, I found her strange and unattractive and wished that A.A. had referred her to someone else. Evidently the stroke had so muddled her mind that she couldn't discuss her drinking. It occurred to me that she probably belonged under the care of a psychiatrist. As I pulled into her driveway, I said, "You've had a lot happen. Have you ever considered professional counseling?"

"No. Never."

"Maybe it would be something to check into."

"I don't need it. A.A. will be sufficient."

For several weeks I drove her to the Friday morning meeting and she called me every morning at exactly nine. She ignored any questions I put to her about her drinking or any mention of the A.A. program and went into monologues on Matt or the stroke or the children or money. At nine when the phone rang, I would think: *Is it or isn't it? Should I or shouldn't I let it go?* I would let the phone ring six or eight times, but finally I would lift the receiver. It never failed to be Carla.

"I don't know what to do about Carla," I told Gene one night at the dinner table. "I'm sick of her calls and her whining. I can't stand her, but I hate myself for thinking it."

"Drop her. You can't help her. She's got a damaged mind."

"But maybe I can help her."

"How? What's your plan?"

"I don't know. But I can't drop a handicapped widow."

"I would. She has family here, doesn't she?"

"Yes."

"I would call them and leave her with them. She's not your responsibility."

But I felt she was.

A few days later on a Saturday morning at about eight, the bedside phone rang. Gene rolled over, answered it, and handed it to me. "It's Carla," he muttered.

"What is it, Carla?" I groaned out. "I'm not up yet."

"I need you to come right now. It's important."

"I'm still half-asleep."

"I wouldn't call if it weren't extremely important."

I went, all the while thinking myself a fool for rushing over, yet worrying that she might have a serious problem.

Carla greeted me with a placid look, not at all the look of a person in trouble.

"Why did you call?" I asked.

In answer she bent forward over the coffee table and rummaged through a clutter of pop cans, glasses, and magazines. "Here it is," she said and pulled a piece of lined notebook paper from under a cola can. She then went through the same clutter, found her reading glasses, put them on, and held up the paper. "This is why I called."

"That? What is it?"

"It's my will."

"Did you write it?"

"I wrote it out last night."

In wonder at the crumpled, messy paper, I couldn't take my eyes from it. "Why?"

"Because I've got cancer."

"Cancer—Carla!"

"I've got primary carcinoma of the liver—malignant hepatoma." She was speaking in the detached manner of a doctor discussing a patient. "It's one of the most virulent types of cancer. I've been given four months to live."

I was stunned that she would soon die, amazed at her matter-of-fact manner. "Can't they do something? Isn't there some treatment—radiation or something like that?"

"No. It's too advanced."

"How long have you known?"

"Two months."

No wonder she had been behaving oddly. Anyone would. I felt terrible. "You're taking it so well," I said. "I couldn't handle it."

"What else can I do? I'm living one day at a time like they say in A.A."

"But isn't there something the doctors can—"

"Nothing can be done," she interrupted. She cleared her throat and pushed her reading glasses high up on her nose. She held up the will. "I'd like you to listen please."

Although I tried to concentrate, I was upset and only caught snatches: the children would live with her brother; the house would be sold, with the proceeds put in trust for the children; Davey, her five-year-old, would get the dog.

When she finished, she said, "I called you because I want your opinion. Have I been fair to everyone?"

"I think so." But I wondered if the messy paper would hold up in court. "Shouldn't you have a lawyer go over it?"

"I intend to. This isn't the final draft. It's ridiculous to waste my lawyer's time until I'm certain what I'm doing with my property."

CHAPTER XV

Five days later Carla was asking, "Since Davey is getting the dog, should Brenda get the cat?"

"That seems fair."

"Should I trust my china to the children or leave it to my brother?"

"I'm not sure. Maybe he could keep it for the children."

This was the fourth time I'd been over this week. I had been listening to revisions of Carla's will; she was determined to get it in perfect order.

"Is it almost all set?" I asked.

"Almost. Just a few little details."

I considered her remarkable. Given the same circumstances, I was sure I would fold.

Then on Saturday afternoon Vivian, Carla's seventeen-year-old daughter, came to my house. She was a plain girl with a high forehead and small, gray eyes. I brought her to the living room, where she hunched up on the edge of a chair and crossed her legs at the knees and ankles. She was wound up like a spring, apparently very nervous. I wondered as to her mission. Had Carla's cancer taken a turn for the worse? Though Carla and I had not discussed it, I assumed the older children knew of the cancer.

In an attempt to calm Vivian, I said, "Do you like going to Finneytown High?"

"It's okay," she said in a monotone.

"It's hard to move in the middle of high school."

She nodded.

"I never had to do that. We always lived in Elmhurst when

I was in high school. That's near Chicago."

"Mrs. Canfield," she said, then broke off. Her eyes filled with tears and she looked down at her lap. "I've come about Mom."

"Yes?"

"She . . . " The tears ran down her cheeks. "I don't know how to say it."

"Just say it, honey."

"I overheard Mom reading you her will. I heard her tell you about her cancer of the liver. She doesn't have any cancer."

I didn't believe Vivian. She had lost her father, was losing her mother, and was now denying truth because she couldn't cope. I went to her, sat on the arm of her chair, and put my hand on her shoulder. I said, "Your mom's very sick, but she's being brave about it."

"She isn't sick."

"I know her condition."

"Mrs. Canfield, please let me explain."

I nodded and Vivian explained.

Carla had invented the cancer. And this was not the first time she had done so. Twice she had become an emotional leech, attaching herself to a Hyde Park neighbor each time. Carla's brother had stepped in with the truth in each instance. When confronted by her brother, Carla would say, "I only wanted to have a friend."

Vivian now gave me an earnest look. "You do believe me?"

After that story, of course I did.

"I'm sorry Mom did this to you," Vivian said. "I came over so you wouldn't be worrying about her."

"It's okay," I said. "Alcoholics often do things like that." I hated being taken advantage of; it always sent my emotions flying. But I had to try to put aside my feelings for Vivian's sake.

She uncrossed her ankles and knees, relaxing now that I had been told and had reacted somewhat calmly.

"Do you think Mom's an alcoholic?" she asked.

"I would think so—she goes to A.A."

"She doesn't drink much."

"How much does she drink?"

"Once in a while she has a glass of wine, but not very often."

Stunned, I blurted out. "No wonder she never wanted to discuss the A.A. program."

Vivian crossed her ankles and legs again.

"Why in the world did she go?" I asked.

"Maybe she was looking for friends."

"I think she needs help. She should see a psychiatrist. Why don't you call your uncle and have him take her to one?"

"She doesn't like psychiatrists."

"Has your uncle tried to get her to one?"

"I don't think so."

"Her behavior is bizarre. She needs something more than she's getting."

"My uncle says she acts like she does because of the stroke, and because she misses Dad."

"Then, he thinks she'll quit all this?"

"Yes."

I didn't know what to think. But I could feel my anger at Carla building.

Soon Vivian rose to leave. The moment the door closed behind her, I let go of my emotions and paced the living room. When I thought about the untold hours I had listened to that woman whine about her circumstances, I could have screamed. And I'd spent the entire week grieving over her phony cancer and her phony will! The woman was unbelievable. She was a horrendous liar. She had deceived me from beginning to end. She was . . . My thoughts hissed to a halt.

I ran to the phone. That woman was going to get a piece of my mind. I dialed and she answered. "Muriel here," I said, feeling my voice bite.

"Vivian just told me she was over. I'm sorry about what I—"

"You're a liar."

"But you must understand. It's been hard with Matt gone. I've been lonely."

"Don't ever call me again."

"It's not been easy—"

"I mean it. I don't ever want to hear your voice again!" I shouted and slammed down the receiver.

Hours after my call to Carla, I tossed in bed, unable to sleep. Yelling at Carla had been like slapping a baby. I hated myself. She had wanted love and I had given anger. I hated that I had been so merciless, but I couldn't call her in the morning and apologize and begin our relationship again. I wanted no part of this whiny, disturbed woman. I didn't like her and I couldn't envision a future of day after day of her. I started to cry.

And not knowing why I was getting up, I swung out of bed and felt my way through the bedroom and into the long, narrow hall that led to the kitchen. Rather than snap on a light, I trailed my fingers along the row of closet doors on the left and the draperies covering the three windows on the right. In the kitchen I snapped on the light over the sink and pulled open the door to the cabinet under the sink.

Then I knew why I had gotten up; I wanted a bourbon. But I wasn't in Elmhurst, I was in Finneytown—and this cabinet only contained bottles of cleaning solution and furniture wax. Frightened that I might go to the storage shed where Gene kept the liquor, I quickly snapped off the light and started down the hall.

At the window I pulled back the draperies and looked into the hall of the house across the driveway. There was a soft glow coming from the hall, a night-light. The glow gave me a warm feeling about their house and somehow made me think of God. With regret I realized that I hadn't prayed for a long time. I put my arms on the sill and bent my head. "Dear God," I said. "please take away this feeling that I want a drink and keep me sober."

I felt some peace, as if He might have heard, and I went to bed and slept.

The next day I had no desire to drink. I didn't call Carla that day, nor the next day, nor the next week, nor during the next months. When I thought about her, I would dislike myself and sometimes get an image of the liquor cabinet in Elmhurst. But then I would think: *You did the best you could have for her. More than most would have. All those hours and hours you spent. In the end your anger will help her. It'll startle her into being truthful, like it startled Bonnie and helped her get sober.*

During those same months, it became my practice to pray each night: "Dear God, please keep me sober." For I remembered that night I had felt His nearness at the window. In addition, I sensed God's interest and believed He would help me work through the Twelve Steps of the A.A. program. I didn't start going to church or reading stacks of religious literature, but I did read a few books written by Catherine Marshall. I prayed only at night. I had the sense of God's hand only in my sobriety. But that relationship with God seemed sufficient. I wasn't particularly happy. *But*, I thought, *with God's help, if I stay sober long enough, I'll find happiness.*

In this same period of time, I felt tired and started to take two- to three-hour afternoon naps. I became thin, my weight dropping from 118 to 108. By February, five months after I met Carla, my sweaters and skirts sagged. It didn't concern me that I was tired and thin; rather, I enjoyed the naps and liked the slimmed-down look.

Then in mid-February I went to have my annual physical examination. I didn't think to mention the fatigue and weight loss. But when Dr. Rose finished the exam, he glanced at my chart and said, "You've lost some weight. Have you been dieting?"

"No," I said.

He nodded and left me to dress.

A few minutes later he came back, sat behind his desk, and motioned me to a chair by his desk. He pushed up his bifocals and studied a piece of paper in his hand. "We've got the urine report. Nancy ran it while you dressed. You're spilling some sugar."

"Is it much sugar? Does it look serious?"

"I doubt it's serious. I'll schedule you for a glucose tolerance test; then we'll know the exact situation."

"Isn't weight loss a sign of diabetes?"

"Yes," he said. "But let's not jump to a diagnosis until we have the tests."

I did have diabetes, a mild case—the reason for the weight drop and fatigue. Dr. Rose prescribed Orinase—an oral tablet which heightened the secretion of insulin—and an 1800-calorie diabetic diet, which was high in carbohydrates and low in fat and protein. Too much fat could harm my circulatory system; too much protein, my kidneys. The Orinase would take care of the carbohydrates.

The day I received the diagnosis, I asked Gene, "Why

me?" He had just been to the drugstore and was standing inside the kitchen door, wiping his snow-caked shoes on a throw rug. He handed me a small brown bag, in it my first bottle of Orinase. I took out a tablet and swallowed it. "I'll be on these the rest of my life. I'll be a slave to my diet. I won't be able to eat candy or desserts. I can't drink—"

"You can't drink anyhow."

"I know, but now I'm cornered into it. Now I can't drink, or else."

"Wasn't it always 'or else'?"

"Maybe, but I couldn't see it so clearly."

Gene slipped off his coat and headed for the coat closet in the long hall. I followed. "Diabetes can be serious," I said. "Diabetics can get gangrene. They can lose their toes, sometimes their legs."

"Not those with mild cases."

"Mine could get worse."

"And you could get flattened by a truck tomorrow."

Gene's philosophy was lost on me—knowing the improbability of a disaster tomorrow was of no comfort today. I hated being a diabetic.

I felt sorry for myself. But I could not afford the feeling; it might bring me to drinking.

A few days later, I began to consider going to work: a job would keep my mind from diabetes; I had the time—the children were in school; but maybe most important of all, I needed to prove I had worth. But I might not prove it, for I had quit college. And I had struggled and almost gone under at the chemical laboratory. And I was an alcoholic. Essentially, I was a failure.

Therefore, I was surprised to find myself remembering the suave Mrs. Smith and thinking that I would like to try real estate. I wondered at the idea, for I was a failure and I was not suave and I was apparently considering more of a job than I could handle.

But Gene thought not. He encouraged me to try.

I did.

At first it seemed that Gene was wrong; I was heading fast for failure. After I passed the state licensing exam, I went to work for Darcey Realtors, a small firm with twelve agents, the count including the two owners and me. And while Mrs.

Smith over at Blackburn Realtors sold house after house, I strove to sell just one house. Six months passed, and I sold nothing.

A tomato plant brings forth tomatoes, I thought, *and a failure brings forth failures.*

Toward the end of my sixth month at Darcey's, I put in an exhausting day. In the morning I hurried the children through breakfast and dressing, helped them gather up notebooks and lunches, and waved them off to school. I then raced through my housework and rushed off to a sales meeting at Darcey's, which culminated in a tour of the week's six new house-listings. In the afternoon I showed nine houses to a young couple, among them a house which they raved about. Hoping to write a purchase contract, I took them back to my office and into the conference room. There, in dismay, and almost in tears, I listened to the young man say, "I think we ought to hold off for a year or two and save up a bigger down payment." After that, I cleaned off my desk, drove home (fortunately only a two-mile trip), and dragged into the kitchen.

On the counter were eggshells, toast crumbs, puddles of milk, and splatters of grease. Gene and the children were at the table eating fried eggs, bacon and toast, and drinking tall glasses of milk.

"It's a mess," I said. "I'm too tired to clean it."

"Don't give me that!" Gene snapped. "It's dirty because *I* cooked."

"Did you make me something?" With his snappy attitude I doubted he had.

"There's bacon on the table and an egg in the pan."

I stared into the pan with dismay.

"How long has it been there?"

"Ten minutes."

"It's cold and hard."

"It would've been hot if you'd gotten home on time. This is the third day in a row you've come in late. You should make it a point to be here."

"I don't get on you about being late to dinner when you're tied up in a meeting."

"That's different. Mine's a job."

"So's mine," I said roughly, at once both crushed and angry, feeling like throwing the rubbery egg at him.

"A job's something you do for money."

That did it. "Money isn't the measure of a job!" I yelled, and ran from the kitchen. I dashed for the bedroom and threw myself on the bed, burying my face in the pillow.

In a second Gene's hand was on my shoulder. "Go away," I said, my voice muffled by the pillow. I lifted my head so that he could clearly hear me and shouted, "Get out of here!"

"I'm sorry."

"You can't be sorry that fast. Not when you act like you think my job's volunteer work."

He kissed my neck and whispered, "Forgive me. Your job's hard work."

He pulled me up and wrapped me in his arms, so obviously sorry that I forgave him. "You're probably right," I said. "I can't call it a job."

"Yes, you can, gal."

"What gets me—" my eyes filled with tears—"is that I'm the worst agent at Darcey's, and Darcey's is one of the smallest agencies in town. That makes me about the worst agent in Cincinnati."

"Look, I'm the one that thought you could make it and I still do."

"I don't think I can."

"You can, gal. Give it some time."

Within days of Gene's encouragement, I began to sell. The young couple, who had almost put me in tears, decided to purchase the bi-level house over which they had raved. I earned $315 commission. And the sales continued. Although I was not a top money earner like Mrs. Smith, I was soon earning $800 a month, a good wage in the early seventies. But my goal was to keep improving my sales skills until I was making $12,000-$15,000 a year.

My salary for today and my potential for tomorrow gave me some self-esteem. In addition, I got a wonderful high, much like I had once gotten from a couple of cocktails, when a client signed an agreement to purchase. The same high came when a home owner signed a listing contract. And at a house closing, when the attorney handed me the commission check, I felt my ego swell. And at the office, when Mr. Darcey told me I had sales talent, I rejoiced and felt great pride in myself.

Gene and I saved all of my commissions and a little of his

salary. Fifteen months after I began selling, we had a sizable amount of money in our savings account and decided to buy a larger house, one with eight rooms, not seven, one with a basement, not on a slab—one with a more expensive look in a better neighborhood.

So we bought a new eight-room colonial on Redmill Drive, a new street with all new colonials, about a mile from Fountainbleau Terrace. The eight rooms included three large bedrooms and a very large master bedroom that had a dressing room with a vanity and a bath with flocked wallpaper. There was a long family room with a fireplace, a pegged oak floor, and a sliding door leading to a redwood deck. Fronting the house were five square pillars, not as large as the ones that Carla had said graced her house, but still large enough to give the house a little elegance.

Though I wasn't entirely aware of it, I had a sense that the house was an expression of me; it had to be perfect. Thus I spent $4,000 on new furniture and carpeted the living and dining room in a sandy-color carpet that exactly matched the furniture. Gene hung sandy antique-satin draperies in the living room that blended perfectly with the carpet and furniture. Outside we planted flowering dogwoods beside the deck, English ivy along the east wall of the house, and cotoneaster in front of the square pillars.

We emptied the savings account.

While all this was going on, I didn't think of myself as displaying materialism, but as displaying good taste. For, if questioned, I would have said that material possessions were not important. Books and real estate and children were important. Materialistic people had selfish spirits and minds.

In the rush of buying and moving, I forgot about God and prayer.

Then, in August of that summer, I received a letter from Laurie Masters, a friend who lived in Elmhurst and who had been a high school classmate. Laurie wrote that she was attending a series of meditation classes. There she had learned how to relax her mind and body and contact spirits, which she believed were emissaries of God. As a result, she felt in harmony with the universe and at one with God. She wrote, "Do you contact the spirits?"

I didn't, of course. But when I had been a student at the

University of Illinois, I had tried to contact them several times. My roommate, a Spiritualist who believed she had a spirit guide, had encouraged me to invite spirits to appear. At the same time she urged me to watch for a person's aura, the color or colors that surrounded his body in a glowing outline. I tried both unsuccessfully. Because I wasn't convinced that there was a spiritual realm, I wasn't disappointed that I didn't see spirits and auras.

Laurie closed her letter with, "How do you feel about all this? Please write."

I laid aside Laurie's letter with a feeling of regret; she was near God and I wasn't. I saw clearly that in the rush of selling real estate and furnishing our house, I had replaced God with materialism. I disliked myself for it. I missed God.

Though I wasn't sure that spirits existed, I wished I could believe that they did so that I could be as close to God as Laurie. Fortunately, I could talk the matter over with her in a few days. For at the end of the week the children and I would be driving to my parents' for a week's visit.

CHAPTER XVI

At the end of the week in the late afternoon, the children and I arrived at my childhood home in Elmhurst. After kissing Mom and Dad, I made a quick study of Dad. His mouth was firm, his blue eyes clear, his hands steady. He was sober, between binges. *It will be a good visit*, I thought with relief. Dad wouldn't be slumped at the kitchen table, drinking scotch and telling the children about "good Old Henry." And Mom wouldn't be crying and telling me that she couldn't stand one more minute of Dad's drinking. (Mom had stopped drinking seven years ago.)

That day there was no time to phone Laurie Masters, but in the morning I went upstairs to the family room and dialed her number. I tended to use this upstairs phone rather than the one downstairs because the family room was cozy, my favorite room in the house.

Laurie answered, and after several minutes of general conversation, I told her I had gotten her letter and asked if I could attend her meditation class.

"It's finished," she said. "But some of the students are starting a meditation club. We're going to meet every week at my house. You're welcome to come."

"Are you planning to contact spirits like you did at the meditation class?"

"Yes."

"You really believe in them, don't you?"

"Yes—do you?"

"Not exactly. But I was impressed that you felt that spirits

"You must know the Bible pretty well," I said.

"Have you ever read it?"

"No. I heard some of it in Sunday school, but that's it."

"For a new Christian, John's a good book to read."

"I don't know. Isn't the Bible tedious reading?"

"No, it's not. In fact, it's God's word to you."

Though I still thought it would be boring, to be polite I said, "Maybe I'll try it, then."

"You won't be bored," Laurie said with such conviction that I said, "Okay. I'll try it today."

So shortly after I hung up, I began reading John and soon came to John 3:16: "For God so loved the world, that he gave his only begotten Son, that whosoever believeth in him should not perish, but have everlasting life."

In the past, at Sunday school, I had memorized the verse. Then there had been no understanding, but now I understood and I cried as I saw the magnitude of God's gift of love, of salvation, of eternal life.

"Thank You," I said.

I loved the Book of John and was not bored, and I read until it was time to make the urine test.

Then in the bathroom beside the family room, I excitedly set up the test tube on the back rim of the sink. When the mix was ready, I dropped in a Clinitest tablet and watched it fizzle up and settle. Blue would indicate no sugar.

So far the mix was blue. But that didn't guarantee a negative result; often when the mix settled and the test tube was shaken, the color changed to green, indicating some sugar.

I picked up the test tube and shook it. The mix remained blue. Negative. *I'm probably healed*, I thought with joy.

I set the test tube in the sink, then ran to the phone, and called Laurie. "I'm probably healed," I blurted. I told her that I had skipped the Orinase, eaten the strudel, and tested. "I should've had a high positive reading, but I didn't. I guess I shouldn't say I'm healed until I run a few more tests, but I really think I am."

"Praise the Lord," she said.

"Just think," I almost sang out, "God's probably healed me."

I soon hung up, and though tempted to run to Mom with the news, I decided with her skepticism it would be best to wait until I was absolutely certain. The next morning the test was again negative. Thus certain of the healing, in the late morning I went to Mom in the kitchen.

She was at the table, writing out a grocery list. As I sat across from her, she asked, "Do you want anything from the store?"

For years I had craved a piece of my favorite dessert, yellow cake with whipped cream frosting. "A whipped cream cake. The kind you used to get that had the pecans on the top." I could almost taste the cake.

"You've been ignoring your diet since yesterday," she snapped. "Are you trying to kill yourself?"

"No—I'm not. It's not how it seems. Something's happened." I began my first Christian testimony. I felt such wonder that first time I testified. My love for Christ was new and I wanted to speak of Him in just the right way. *She mustn't categorize this as a type of spiritualism*, I thought. Finally I came to the point where I had rushed home and up to the bedroom. "I knelt beside the bed," I said. "I gave my life to Jesus."

I paused and studied Mom a moment. The skin on her forehead was drawn tight, her lips were pursed. *She's not understanding or accepting*, I thought. "What's wrong?" I asked.

"You sound like a fanatic."

But I continued, and as I did, her eyes narrowed in disbelief and hardened with suspicion.

When I finished, she said, "Before you go flying off like this, you should see a doctor."

"I will—when I get home. But two urine tests certainly don't lie. You can't refute the facts. I'm healed."

Maybe I spoke a little high-handedly, for Mom pulled herself up straight and, gathering all the disbelief and suspicion of before, plus some, gave me a terrible look. In response and without thinking, I said, "You're looking at me as if you think I'm full of—."

I fell back against my chair in dismay. How could I have capped my testimony with that word? Mom hated foul language and never used it. She would now hate Christianity; think it as disgusting as the word.

She reacted immediately. Tears came to her eyes. She jumped up from the chair and sped past the table and through the door leading to the basement.

I ran after her and met her at the double sink next to the washing machine. She turned her back to me and folded her arms over her chest. Her shoulders shook, and I knew she was crying. I put my arms around her shoulders and said, "I'm sorry. Please forgive me."

"Let's just forget it," she said.

"I can't until you forgive me."

"I don't want to discuss it."

"But, Mom—"

"Please. I don't want to hear another word on the subject."

Knowing that I could say no more, I dropped my arms and left her. The remainder of the day, we were careful with each other—Mom, because she was obviously still hurt; I, because I didn't want to hurt her again. For me it was an unhappy situation; I feared that one word would always keep Mom from Jesus.

A few days later, despite the experience with Mom, I testified to Debbie and Douglas, now thirteen and nine. We were in the family room. Debbie was lying on her back on the floor with her knees up, and Douglas was mostly on his back near her feet. They listened closely.

When I finished, Debbie said, "I know about Jesus. I gave Him my life at Bible camp."

Amazed, I went after the facts. "That camp you went to with your friend, Kay, a couple of years ago? The one in the country that you went to every day for a week?"

"Yes."

"Me, too," said Douglas, popping up to a sitting position. "When Debbie came home one day, she told me about Jesus and I asked Him into my heart."

First Debbie, now him. I was stunned and could only manage to whisper, "You did? Why didn't you tell me?"

"I did," he said.

"I did, too," said Debbie. "Don't you remember?"

The fact that my children were Christians was hitting me hard now, and tears came as I strained to remember. At that moment I would have traded the past to remember, but I couldn't. I did remember Debbie at five, kneeling beside my bed and telling God that she loved Him. And I remember the day Douglas had seen the angel. But their Christian testimonies were forgotten in the way I had of forgetting trivia.

"I don't remember."

Debbie's eyes widened, as if amazed that I could forget. "Darling, please forgive me. If only you could know how I feel now. Your news is the best news I've ever had."

She moved close and wrapped her arms around me.

In a minute I let her go and hugged Douglas. Then he asked, "Did Dad just become a Christian too?"

"Not that I know of."

"I think he will."

An odd remark, I thought, but gave it no pause, for Debbie was saying, "We pray for Dad."

"You do?"

"Every day," said Douglas.

"Then you prayed for me?"

They nodded. At their love tears came again. "And I met Jesus." I paused, understanding Douglas' odd remark. "And Dad will too, because God answers prayer."

They nodded again.

That evening in response to my testimony, I discovered that Donny was not a Christian and was not interested in Christianity.

So when the two-week stint was over, we boarded a plane for Grande Prairie. We were not all Christians, and we were going home to Gene, who neither believed in God nor Christ. God had changed my life during that visit, but Mom remained unmoved. She believed in God, but couldn't tolerate the mention of Christ.

CHAPTER XX

I was sitting close to the edge of the couch, telling Gene about my experience and hoping to lead him to salvation. He was stretched out on the gold-striped chair with his legs out like poles against the carpet. It was early evening, several hours after the children and I had flown into the Grande Prairie airport.

Close to the end of my testimony, I took a reading of Gene's flat eyes and his often-raised eyebrow, and realized that he wasn't coming to a belief in Christ—or my healing. So when I finished, I said. "You obviously don't believe any of this."

He studied me. "Does all this make you happy?"

"Yes."

"Then I'm glad you found something inspirational."

"Is that all you have to say about what I've said? You could at least say you're glad I'm healed."

"I am, if that's the case."

"It is the case."

He nodded politely, then said, "While you've been gone, I've found something inspirational too."

He explained that he had found my copy of the Edgar Cayce biography. He was now halfway through it and was impressed with Cayce's supernatural ability and his philosophy. "You read the book, right?" Gene asked.

"Yes, but I don't believe in Cayce's philosophy."

Nonetheless, Gene began to review what he had read, highlighting the two points that most impressed him: first, Cayce's ability to sink into a trance, telepathically diagnose a

167

patient's illness, and prescribe a treatment; second, Cayce's ability to prophesy, to actually plug into the Universal Mind, a register of the past, present and future.

I interrupted, "I'm not a Cayce fan. He's not accurate. A lot of his prophecies never come to pass."

"And a lot do. But that's not the point I'm getting to. The point is that Cayce was in touch with a Universal Mind, a power that might flow from God."

"That's a strange statement from an agnostic. You're almost saying that you believe in God."

"People's ideas change."

"Have yours? Do you believe in God?"

"Yes, I might—a little. The book's started me thinking."

"But you're not understanding rightly. God's not the source of the Universal Mind. I don't believe in the Universal Mind."

"You would if you saw someone plug into it."

"I don't think so."

Ignoring my comment, Gene said, "Not everyone has Cayce's ability to plug in, but those that do should be able to control matter. They should be able to put out light bulbs with their minds—"

"Put out light bulbs! Control matter! Cayce never did that."

"I'm not saying he did. I'm just speculating. It's a mind exercise."

It was unusual for logical Gene to speculate, and extraordinary for him to entertain such far-fetched theories. *One thing is clear*, I thought, *he's not interested in You, Jesus.*

Yet, on the other hand, he was granting the existence of God.

I found the direction the discussion was taking disheartening and said, "Excuse me. I guess I'm getting hungry."

I went to the refrigerator and took out the ice cream. "Want a chocolate sundae?" I called back to Gene.

"Yes." He came to me, got out the scoop, and started dipping the ice cream. "Are you sure you can have this? Are you sure you're healed?"

"I'm sure," I said, leaving the matter there, for I didn't want to draw Gene into a discussion of Cayce's healing abilities.

"Did you go to a doctor at your Mom's?"

"No, but I will here. I'm sure the doctor will confirm the healing."

"Then if you're really healed, it could be a case of mind over matter."

I said, my voice dropping with each word, "It's not mind over matter."

Gene caught my mood. "I'm sorry, gal. This Christianity's important to you, isn't it?"

"Yes."

Gene again discussed Cayce and the Universal Mind the next night and for several nights running. He would state that Christ couldn't be proven, thus Christianity was emotional; that the Universal Mind theory could be proven by fulfilled prophecy and was therefore rational. Just a few weeks ago my views were similar to his, and so I now sensed he was feeling his way along the edge of Christianity.

"Give him understanding, Lord," I kept praying with a feeling of excitement.

During the same week, I went to the doctor. He ran a glucose tolerance test, and my blood sugar was normal. Gene was pleased, but thought it either mind over matter or a natural healing.

Then on Saturday night as Gene and I lay in bed, I said, "I'll be going to church in the morning."

"Where?"

"The white brick one. The one close to town on 100th Avenue." I had picked the church because it was familiar; I drove past it almost daily. Remembering back to the gloomy Dr. Kinder of my teen years who gave social/political sermons, and the intellectual church which Gene and I visited, I hoped that I had chosen a church that preached Christianity.

"What kind of a church is it?"

I gave him the denomination, then said, "I hope it's one where the people love Christ."

"I guess you know I won't be going."

"I didn't think you would."

"You understand that I'd feel like a hypocrite."

"Yes."

In the morning when the alarm jangled, I swung to the side of the bed and shoved on my slippers. "Church?" Gene mumbled, then bunched up his pillow and covered his eyes with his arm. "See you later."

Assuming he planned to go back to sleep, I quietly took a brown wool dress from the closet and went to the bathroom. But while I brushed my teeth, instead of a snore, I heard a scrape and a rattle, as if Gene were sliding his change across the dresser and dropping it into his pocket.

Shortly, he was at the bathroom doorway in suit pants, a white shirt, and a tie.

"I thought you weren't going," I said.

"I've changed my mind."

"Why?"

"Because you probably wouldn't want to go alone."

"You'd go because of me?"

"Yes, gal." His voice was gentle, his eyes tender.

His love made my throat catch. "I don't mind going alone."

He stepped to me and kissed my hair. "You're sure?"

"I'm sure."

"Then I guess I'll stay home."

At church, in order to have a clear view of the pulpit, I chose a pew toward the front of the sanctuary and sat behind a child. I was early, and it was several minutes before the pastor, the Reverend Milton Claar, came into the chancel through a side door and stepped up to the pulpit. Trailing after him was a choir of about ten, who filed up to the choir loft directly behind the pulpit.

Although Rev. Claar's face was as smooth as an eggshell, I guessed him to be about fifty, because the skin under his eyes pouched. He was thin and almost bald, with just a fringe of hair ringing the back of his neck. What struck me most, though, was his expression—pinched—as if he had just sucked a lemon or lost a vast sum in the stock market.

Throughout the hymns, prayers, announcements and offering, Rev. Claar retained his pinched expression. And whenever he spoke, his voice was tight and flat. But something happened to him when he began the sermon. His somber eyes took on a faint light and his tight voice loosened and flowed and occasionally soared. Drawn by his voice, I listened with attention.

He based his sermon on the experience of Zacchaeus who had climbed a sycamore tree so that he could view Jesus passing below. He said, "Just as Zacchaeus climbed the sycamore and placed himself high above the crowd, we must each climb our own sycamores and place ourselves in a position where we can best view God. We must climb and surmount our problems. . . . We must climb until we have an unobstructed view of God. . . . We must all climb continually onward and upward." His voice boomed and vibrated through the sanctuary as he concluded with, "Climb!"

Inspired by his vigorous close, I was tempted to begin the climb. But the temptation lasted just a second. For in the past, although I had scraped my knees raw trying to climb sycamores, the attempts had not produced a clearer view of God. It was faith that had given me the view. Faith in Jesus Christ.

I was disappointed in the minister's perspective. Why had he zeroed in on climbing instead of faith? Was his the sermon of a man who loved Jesus? Was it even the sermon of a Christian?

After the benediction, I put my hymnal in the pew rack and stepped into the line waiting to shake hands with the pastor. I was not far back, and in a few minutes I had his hand in mine. As before the sermon, his expression was pinched.

In keeping with his grave nod, I gave him a small smile—and to my surprise, I said, "Is there any chance you could call, because I'd like to share my testimony with you?" Suddenly I gulped with regret. It seemed right that a minister should hear my testimony, then welcome me into Christianity, but wrong that I should choose the pinched Reverend Claar, whose Christianity I questioned. But I had already spoken.

Without hesitation he said, "Of course. Give my secretary a call tomorrow and arrange a date."

A few days later in the early afternoon, the Reverend Claar came. He took the gold-striped chair, squared up his shoulders like the head of a T-square, and spread his long, thin fingers across his knees. The August sun had heated the living room to at least 90 degrees, and in a few minutes perspiration beaded his forehead.

"Are you hot?" I asked.

"I'm a bit uncomfortable."

Reaching behind his chair, I pulled open the sliding balcony doors. "Is that better?"

It was, and after a few minutes of social chatter, I brought in two cups of coffee, sat on the couch, and began my testimony. The man listened attentively, his somber gray eyes always on mine.

When I finished, he said, "Have you had your healing verified with a doctor?"

"Yes. I had a glucose tolerance test several days ago."

"And?"

"My blood sugar's normal."

"Oh," he said, then fell quiet. He tapped his knees with his fingers, and gave me a skeptical look, as if he thought my test results might be in error.

"The test is accurate," I said. "I have no signs of diabetes. I don't take any medication. I don't follow a diabetic diet."

"You sound like one of those Jesus people."

"Which Jesus people?"

"The ones who run around preaching love and peace."

"Is that so wrong?"

"It's overemotional. We've got to be practical. Life's not all joy."

"I know it's not. I haven't had the kind of life that would make me think it was. I've been a drinker, an alcoholic. But there's joy in Christianity. What's wrong with telling people that?"

"Your emotions are way up," he said. "They'll come down with a thump. What goes up must come down."

"I know I'll be down sometimes—but everybody is. It's normal."

His line was leading me quickly toward the conclusion that he wasn't a Christian. For if he were, he would be rejoicing in the way of the angels in heaven. I wanted to ask him bluntly if he were, but in politeness I refrained and asked, "What made you decide to go into the ministry?"

"My parents didn't have much money, and when it came to careers, I—"

The doorbell rang. *Nuts*, I thought, hating the interruption of his answer.

"Excuse me," I said and hurried to the door.

Oh, no! I thought as I opened it and saw Fran swaying in

the hallway of the apartment. She was a member of my A.A. group, a thirty-five-year-old mother of nine illegitimate children. Fran was an Indian. She was tall and stocky and had a square face with a jaw that jutted out presumptuously, as if daring a fight. As was often the case, she was plastered. Her black hair was tangled, her black eyes were blurry, her blouse was stained. And she smelled as sour as a gallon of curdled milk.

Though others and I had tried to help her work through the Twelve Steps, she staggered in and out of A.A. When out, she went on horrendous binges where she drank around-the-clock; spent most of her welfare check on liquor (she was supported solely by Social Welfare); sold furniture and personal possessions; slept with almost any man who would buy her a drink. On the binges she was a negligent, sometimes cruel, mother. Therefore, several times Social Welfare had taken the children and placed them in foster homes. Right now, seven children were in foster homes, one was in prison, one was at home with her.

It was true that when sober, Fran was shy, nervous, guilty over the binges, and that when drunk or sober she was desolate over the loss of her children. But I didn't like her because I couldn't get past her disastrous drunks and nasty personality changes.

"Come in," I said, giving her a bleak look and imagining the minister's reaction to her. He would, of course, be repelled and conclude that people with testimonies like mine gravitated toward friendships with drunken women. This was upsetting, for I had always needed the regard of others.

Fran stepped in, stumbled over nothing, and toppled into the doorjamb. I grasped her arm and led her to a chair. While she dropped into it, I introduced her to the Reverend Claar and identified him as the pastor of the church on 100th Avenue. Without raising an eyebrow, he leaned over, shook her hand, and said pleasantly, "How do you do?"

"Hi. I don't go to your church," she said, matching his pleasant tone and smiling, a rarity when she drank. I had expected a grunt and scowl, and I wondered if she had taken a liking to him.

"I know," he said. "I haven't seen you there."

"I used to go every Sunday with my mother."

"To my church?"

"No, to my church up in Hay River. I used to pray by my bed every night, but I quit going to church." The effort of carrying on a somewhat coherent conversation seemed to be getting to Fran, and she drooped against the wing of the chair. She peered dizzily at the man, as if viewing him from a swaying bridge. "I don't pray much anymore," she said.

"Many don't," he said. "Many have fallen away."

"I've sinned."

"We all do. Perhaps you can discuss your problem with your minister."

"I told you, I quit going to church. I don't have one."

"Then discuss it with me. I'm sure the matter can be set straight."

"I'm too far gone," she said and tears came.

Mr. Claar's somber eyes softened and he said, "Nobody's too far gone." He touched her arm. The compassion he was showing surprised me, and I liked him for it. In a sense, it was like finding a flake of gold in a rock.

"God'll never forgive me."

"He forgave me," I said.

Her mood suddenly shifted to the one I knew best and she flashed out, "What do you know about it?" She held out her chin, as if to fight the point.

"I know something about it. God—"

"I hate God!" she spat. "He treats me like dirt. When's He ever answered my prayers?"

"You don't give Him a chance," I said. "You always do things your own way."

"I've given Him a thousand chances."

The pastor touched her again and for a moment I saw a quality of caring that was not in my grasp. He said, "Then give Him one more."

With the touch, Fran relaxed her chin and quietly quoted an A.A. slogan, "Let go and let God."

"Yes, that's the right idea," he said.

At that point Fran decided to leave.

"I'll drive you," I said.

"Stay," said Fran. "I'll walk."

"I'd be happy to take her," Mr. Claar said.

Fran glared at me. "I told you I'd walk. Nobody takes me."

Mr. Claar stood, and I trailed him to the door, where he paused and told Fran, "Call or stop in if there's ever anything I can do." And to me he said, "Of course, the same goes for you."

"Thank you," I said.

He left and I went to Fran. "I'll take you home now."

"I can walk," she said, standing and swaying, but not taking a step, her feet seemingly bolted to the carpet. I took her arm, tugged, and got her heading for the door. "Let go," she muttered, shaking away my arm and zagging along the carpet and through the door and on out to my car. "I don't want a ride," she said and stepped into the car and fell onto the seat. "Let me out of here," she demanded as we drove away from the apartment.

At her house I helped her from the car and led her into her bedroom and to her bed. She fell in and said, "Get out of here. I'm fine."

Her sheets were filthy, and in disgust I looked down and saw, not Fran, but a dirty turnip sprawled on a dirty sack. In a thorny voice I said, "You're not fine. You need to straighten yourself out and get back to A.A. What kind of mother are you? No wonder Welfare takes your kids."

"Straight from the mouth of a saint!" she spat.

"I'm not a saint. I'm just like anybody else."

Lying there flat on her back, she still managed to draw her eyes into points and give me a look of hate. "You're a white know-it-all."

Not me, I thought. But even as I was thinking I wasn't, I realized that I had been treating Fran as if I were Lake Michigan and she were a piece of scum floating on a wave. "I'm sorry," I said. "You're right."

"You're *right* I'm right!" And in a volley of invective she told me everything else that I was.

"Forgive me," I said. "I just became a Christian. I'm not perfect, but I'm trying to change."

"You're doing a lousy job."

"I know, but I'm trying."

"Go practice on somebody else." I didn't move to leave. "Get out of here!" she screeched.

I left, and with tears falling onto my blouse, I drove away, hating myself for treating Fran like scum. I recalled the bridge party at Paula's when I had realized that my thoughts were so self-directed that I couldn't love Gene. In the same way I couldn't love others. I saw my self-directed thinking brought on two antithetical givens: (1) I was the only person I loved; (2) I hated myself and needed the esteem of others in order to esteem myself.

I lived just blocks from Fran, and in a minute I was at our apartment parking lot. I pulled into a spot but didn't leave the car, because into my mind was coming a list of people I had hindered or harmed.

Fran: Harmed.

Carla: Hindered. She had needed a friend and I had not been a friend.

Mom: Harmed. My use of foul language while testifying had destroyed her chance of becoming a Christian.

Ellen: Harmed, badly damaged. I had introduced her to alcohol, then taught her to drink. She was now an alcoholic.

Donny, Debbie, Douglas: Harmed. Emotionally damaged in the wake of my drinking, in the tense years of my sobriety.

Gene: Harmed. I hadn't valued him. I had fluctuated between not loving him and loving him with a love as feeble as an old woman's last breath.

The damage seemed irreparable and my stomach felt queasy until I remembered the Lord and the A.A. slogan Fran had quoted—*Let go and let God.* "Forgive me, Lord," I said. "Forgive me for hurting Fran . . . Carla . . . Mom . . . Ellen . . . the children . . . Gene. I give them to You, Lord. Care for them, Lord."

I felt Christ's love, His forgiveness—and I knew that in Him I could learn to love. "Teach me to love, Lord. Show me how to be Fran's friend.

"Change me, Lord.

"I love You, Lord."

Later, after I was in bed, the light turned off and the drapery shut, when it was dark and it would be easier to say what I wanted to say, I said to Gene, "I've got something to tell you."

"Yes?"

"I've never loved you like I should."

"No, you haven't."

"I'm sorry for it."

"What can I say, gal?"

"Nothing. But I want you to know that I've prayed. I believe God can help me change."

"Well . . ." Gene said, evidently uncertain as to a response.

I was uncertain as to how to continue, so I said, "Good night. Have a good sleep."

But I was certain that a change had begun, for how else could I have said what I just said?

CHAPTER XXI

A couple of days later from the gold-striped chair, Gene was saying, "That kind of church preaches nothing but hellfire and damnation."

"The minister's sermon wasn't anything near that."

"An exception, probably."

"I doubt it." I had just come from a church on the west side of town, one that was recommended by a friend of a friend. Despite the Reverend Claar's compassion to Fran, I had decided against returning to his church.

"Then what was the sermon about?" Gene asked.

"The believer's inheritance. For his text he used verses from Romans 8."

"What did the verses say?"

"I don't remember word for word. Just a minute—I'll look." I reached to the coffee table for my Bible, turned to Romans 8, and began scanning the chapter.

After a couple of minutes, Gene broke in with an impatient tone, "Let me have it. I'll read. When I get to them, stop me."

He began and I listened amazed; here was Gene, who never read the Bible, who had developed through Edgar Cayce a strange faith in God, reading the Bible to me.

Although he had started out quietly enough, when he got to Romans 8:37-39, the final verses, his voice picked up volume and power: " 'Nay, in all these things we are more than conquerors through him that loved us. For I am persuaded, that neither death, nor life, nor angels, nor principalities, nor powers, nor things present, nor things to come, nor height, nor depth, nor any other creature, shall be able to separate us from the love of God, which is in Christ Jesus our Lord.' ''

Clearly moved, Gene closed my Bible. His eyes were on his hands, which lay on the Bible. There was power in the moment, but it was Gene's moment. I left him.

That night at 2:00 a.m. the phone rang incessantly until Gene rolled over in bed and picked up the receiver. "Hello. What is it?" he muttered.

"Muriel's asleep . . .

"I don't think so . . .

"I doubt it . . .

"Just a minute." Gene tapped my shoulder.

"I'm not asleep," I said, and sat leaning against the headboard.

Gene cupped the mouthpiece. "It's Fran."

"What does she want?"

"She's plastered. She's at the Riviera Motel and she wants you to come get her and take her home. She's had a fight with Archie."

"I don't know Archie."

"He's obviously another one of her boyfriends. I don't want you to go. I don't want you to get mixed up in it."

"She could be in trouble. Archie could be mean."

"That's not your problem; it's her problem," he said sharply. He was upset and taking this position because he disliked Fran. For him it had been dislike at first sight.

"I've got to go," I said, thinking, *If I go to Fran at this hour, she'll know I've moved from judge to friend.*

"I get it. You're bent on going because you think it's your Christian duty."

"It's not duty; it's for friendship." Gene shook his head as if unable to comprehend the possibility of a friendship with Fran, so I gave him a reason he would understand. "You forget she's an A.A. member. We help each other."

"Some A.A. member. Anyone plastered ninety percent of the time is not an A.A. member."

"She's an A.A. member because she considers herself an A.A. member."

"I think I'm a cat. Am I a cat?"

That comment, every comment since the phone call, his

dislike of Fran at first sight were not reactions I would expect from Gene. Why was he coming down harder on her than he had on me when I drank? Then I remembered the night he had attended the A.A. meeting and had told me that he didn't let others get the best of him. He was a strong person. And suddenly I knew that under that strength and self-sufficiency lay feelings that he didn't see. And his reaction to Fran was an expression of his feelings about me when I drank. How much I had hurt him! For a second the phone in Gene's hand blurred under tears as I saw the person I had been to him.

He evidently read my tears as compassion for Fran and was moved, for he said, "I'll go with you. I don't want you there alone. Who knows what's going on."

We soon were approaching the Riviera Motel, a drab place of sea-green concrete block. We found Fran's room and knocked. "Come in!" she yelled.

We entered a room that was of the same shade of green as the concrete block. Fran was sitting on the edge of a worn couch with her purse hooked over her arm and her sweater by her side. Her yellow blouse was buttoned up to the collar, perhaps an attempt at propriety. "I'm ready," she said. Then instead of standing she glared at Archie, who was hunched on the side of the bed in just his jeans with his thin shoulder blades sticking up like chicken wings.

I moved near Fran on the couch, but Gene stayed at the wall beside the door, as if readying for a fast exit.

"I'm not staying in this room one more minute," said Fran.

"Then let's go," I said.

"The sooner you get out of here, the better!" shouted Archie.

"Which won't be soon enough!" yelled Fran. She gave him a murderous look, then leaned toward me and said confidentially, "If I ever see him again, I'll kill him."

"Just try," said Archie.

"What's wrong?" I asked Fran.

"Don't ask," said Gene.

"Archie hit me," said Fran.

"I hit her because she socked me," said Archie.

The air nearly turned purple in the flurry of name-calling that followed.

Fran then got up, stumbled over to the bed, put the palm

of her hand on Archie's forehead, and pushed him onto his back, an easy matter as she was thirty or forty pounds heavier than he. While he kicked in protest, she moved her hands to his shoulders and pinned him against the sheet.

"Let him go," said Gene, taking several fast strides to the bed.

"Stay out of my business," said Fran, releasing Archie, who moved to the side of the bed and hunched in his shoulders and retracted his neck like a turtle pulling into a shell.

"You called," Gene said. "You made it my business."

"Get out of here. You . . ." In a heat of swearing Fran swooped to the couch for her purse and swung at Gene's head. Gene jumped aside and she missed him by several feet.

Gene's eyes burned with such anger that I knew he held himself from her with great effort. "Cut it out, Fran," I said, hoping to defuse the situation.

"Shut up."

"Leave us alone," said Archie, blinking timidly at the boldness of his command.

"Leave!" yelled Fran.

"Gladly," said Gene.

"Are you coming, Fran?" I said.

"No," said Fran in an even tone, her anger suddenly gone. "I'm staying with Archie." She gave him an affectionate smile, which he returned.

Gene took my arm. "Let's go, Muriel. This is insane."

"This is your last chance," I said to Fran, as we walked to the door. "You're sure you don't want to come?"

"She's staying with her Archie," said Archie, reaching up and plucking at the back of Fran's blouse. She sat beside him and he put his arm across her shoulder.

Gene and I stepped outside and Archie called after us, "Sorry we got you out of bed."

"Shut up," I heard Fran tell him, as I shut the door.

While we walked to the car, Gene muttered in disgust, "Coming here was a wild goose chase."

"Maybe not. Maybe my coming meant something to her."

"It meant nothing. She's not the type that can be helped. She's a waste of your time."

"She's a person," I said, as we came to the car.

Gene didn't comment, but as we got into the car he said,

"You're dead set on helping her?"

"Yes."

"Like you helped Bonnie and Carla?"

"If you're warning me, you don't need to. I was a different person then."

"I wasn't warning. I was thinking that at least you tried."

"What do you mean?"

"I mean, *I've* never tried with anyone."

"That's not true."

"Who?"

"*Me.* You took care of me when I drank. What if you'd given up on me?"

No, he couldn't, I thought. Almost from the moment he met me the summer I was a waitress at Tony's Pizza, he had loved me with a love that seemed God-given.

Gene started the car, and after we started down the highway, he said, "Come here, gal."

I slid over to him and he put his arm over my shoulder. I noted the speedometer, which was five miles under the speed limit. "Can't you speed up?" I asked. "You're allowed to go five over."

"You aren't. You've told me that six hundred times and it's a figment of your imagination."

"It isn't. I've read it."

"Where?"

"I don't know. Somewhere, though, or I wouldn't know it. Everyone I know drives five miles over. There's an unwritten agreement with the police that one can."

"That's bunk."

"Maybe you're right," I said.

He raised his eyebrow in surprise, for he knew I loved to speed. "Maybe Christians shouldn't break the law," I said.

"Nobody should break the law."

We drove into the business district, then turned left onto the road that led to the apartment. I thought about Gene's poky driving, my speeding; how careful he was, how impetuous I was. And I sensed that God had given him to me for a ballast and an anchor; and me to him for a breeze and a sail. I moved closer against his side, appreciating Gene, loving him.

But from experience I knew my love could be gone tomorrow. Yet Gene's wouldn't. Even when angry or exasperated with me, he loved me. I wanted that kind of love for him. "Please teach me, Lord," I prayed silently.

Although it didn't seem so at the time, that night at the Riviera, my friendship with Fran started. The next day she sobered up, and in her shy way she thanked me for coming to the motel. I began to have coffee three or four times a week at her tiny house with its sagging front porch and cracked living room window. I soon knew that I cared for her—and for Eddie, her three-year-old son who lived at home, his dark eyes too large and solemn for his face; and for Archie, who moved in to share her bed.

I found it wasn't so hard to care for a woman who had a lover and a history of lovers, because I had sinned and was forgiven. I also realized that Jesus had shown the same care to the Samaritan woman. The hard part was learning to love Fran's past, the life her drinking had given Eddie and his brothers and sisters. My feelings faltered the most when I considered Eddie's tenuous future.

Just after Fran sobered up, Social Welfare told her that if she drank again, they would place Eddie in a foster home. And they would make sure the placement would be permanent. Even though Fran had lost eight children and could not bear the loss of the last, she allowed Archie to remain—drinking. He wouldn't stop. He was an alcoholic, an ex-roofer supported by Welfare, a man committed to drinking. She would surely drink with him. Eddie would lose his mother; a terrible loss, for he loved her and often trailed her around the house with his teddy bear in his hand.

One night in bed, about three weeks after the trip to the Riviera Motel, I brought the problem to God. "I'm worried, Lord," I prayed. "What should I do? Should I tell Fran to tell Archie to pack up and leave?"

As I prayed, a thought came strongly into my mind. *Just love her.*

I sensed it was God speaking and I thought, *That's all? Shouldn't I take some action?*

Love her.

All right, I thought.

Although I didn't then know Colossians 3:14, my spirit was responding to the principle: "And above all these things *put on* charity [love], which is the bond of perfectness."

I was putting on love, which was an action, and in the action I was acquiring perfection.

Two days later Fran phoned from a friend's house. "Hi, it's Fran," she said belligerently, daring me to challenge that fact.

She was drunk, of course.

"I'm drunk," she spat out.

"I wish you weren't," I said.

"Don't give me that," she growled. Then her voice lowered and became as empty as a burned-out field. "Eddie's gone."

My voice was caught in my throat and I couldn't answer.

"My neighbor, Pat, found him in the street in the middle of the night," she said. "He was in his underpants. He didn't have his shoes on. She called the police, and Social Welfare came and took him this morning."

"Where were you when Pat found Eddie?"

"Drinking with Archie." She paused, then said, "They'll never give him back. I'm all alone."

"You've got Archie," I said bitterly and hung up, disliking her intensely.

But then the thought returned—*love her.*

It doesn't do any good. Eddie's gone. She's drunk.

Love her.

I don't understand. I should've stepped in and done something.

Just love her.

Okay, I thought, because I sensed this was God, whom I loved and whom I wanted to obey.

CHAPTER XXII

By September the impact of Romans 8 had worn away, and Gene was in the gold-striped chair saying, "I would never consider Christianity. In it, two and two add up to eight. I think in terms of logic, not fantasy."

I was heading from the kitchen toward the couch with a chocolate chip cookie in my hand. It was ten o'clock, and a few minutes before I had come in from my Thursday evening Bible study. Besides that study, I attended a Wednesday morning women's Bible study and Sunday services at the church on the westside. Later, in favor of those activities, I found myself declining some party invitations and even A.A. meetings. And as I further studied the Bible, I became more attracted to the truth in it than to the philosophy in the Twelve steps of A.A. When I skipped a meeting, I had no qualms, for I would think, *I've got a better chance of staying sober under truth than under philosophy.*

I sat on the couch, and rather than eat the cookie, I set it on the coffee table and answered Gene. "And what's so logical about your Universal Mind theory?"

"Nothing. I'm giving it up."

"Really?"

"I was off on a tack."

"Do you think God was part of the tack?"

"No. That part might be real. Someone had to start up the universe. Someone was the beginning before the beginning. That might be God."

"It was," I said.

"You never back off, do you?"

"Would you like it if I did? Would you like it if I gave up Christianity?"

Not that I could have, but the answer would give me a peek into Gene's spirit. He didn't answer immediately, but sipped his coffee and looked at the writing desk to his right. Finally he said, "No, I hope you never give it up."

A few days later when I saw Douglas at the kitchen table with his labeler, I had no idea that he was working on a project to bring Gene to Christ. It simply looked as if he were printing strips of tape, as he often did. Then shortly he called me to the table to see what he had printed, and I looked down to a row of three strips which read: "Jesus loves Dad; Jesus wants Dad; Jesus has Mom and Debbie and Douglas."

"They're for Dad," he said.

"What do you mean?"

"I'm going to put them around for him," he said and grabbed them and jumped up. He then attached a strip to my bedroom door, one to the bathroom mirror, and one to the front door, the side facing the outside hallway.

"Do you like them?" he asked when he had finished.

I choked up at this expression of love for his father and said, "Yes, I love them."

When Gene came home and saw the tapes, he said, "They're nice." He laughed as if it were a joke.

But in the next few days I saw that it wasn't a joke with him. Almost wherever he went, he faced a tape, yet he never took one down. It was as if he considered them holy.

About a week after the tapes went up, I saw how very holy the tapes were to Gene. A friend of mine came for coffee and questioned him about the tapes. Gene said, "My son put them up. He's a Christian. He wants me to be one, too."

A few weeks later, a letter came from Mom. As I opened the envelope, my eyes were fixed on the hoarfrost on the trees beside the balcony. But soon I gave the letter my full attention as I read that my testimony and healing had startled her into thinking about Jesus Christ. She was becoming interested in Christianity and healing, and tonight she would attend a healing service with Laurie Masters. "I'm hoping to find out what brought about your healing," she wrote. "Laurie's picking me up at 8:00."

All excited, I checked the postmark. Her tonight was six nights ago. It could be that Mom had gone to the meeting and had given her life to Jesus. Right now, Mom could be a Christian.

I wanted to phone immediately, but the toll was high, so I waited until the night rates began. Then without much prelude, I said, "Mom, I got you're letter. Did you get to the meeting?"

"I went. Laurie picked me up—"

"What did you think of it?" I was impatient to get my answer.

"I liked it."

"What happened?"

"There were several healings. A crippled woman got out of her wheelchair and walked for the first time in years."

"Anything else?"

"A man who hadn't—"

"Mom! You know what I mean."

"Yes—I'm a Christian."

I started to speak, but my throat tightened and I cried. My mom was a Christian! God had brought her beyond my testimony to Jesus. *Thank You, God*, I thought. *Oh, thank You.*

"I thought you never would," I finally said.

In a dazzling sweep God brought most of my family to Christ. After Mom there was Ellen, the sister who was an alcoholic. By the time Ellen was twenty-eight, she had married, given birth to a girl, divorced, and tried to kill herself—she wanted to die because she hated her drinking and she hated herself. One night she had swallowed twenty aspirins and twenty tranquilizers, curled up on the couch, and waited to die. Instead of dying, she vomited. Her weak stomach saved her.

In a few months Ellen was all set to try again. This time she would not vomit. This time she would die. But unaccountably, before swallowing a handful of pills, she found herself praying, "I'm going to kill myself. I don't think You can stop me." Although she felt as if she had spoken to the wall, God stopped her. Into her spirit came a feeling that Jesus Christ—whom Mom loved, whom Muriel loved—loved *her*. He would give her the strength to live.

188

She wrote me: "God saved me from killing myself—the mercy of Him who saved me."

After Ellen, Chris became a Christian. She was my elegant sister, the one who had taken her five children to Sunday school and whose husband, Bruce, had pledged a percentage of his income to the church. Though she had become irregular at times in her church attendance, she believed in church, God, good morals, helping others, truth—and so she thought she was a Christian.

That was until she heard Mom and Ellen talking about Jesus Christ as they never had, and she saw a light in their eyes that they'd never had. Impressed, she prayed, "God, something's missing in my life. Is it Jesus Christ?" A strong urge came to read her Bible. In it she found that it was Jesus Christ who would complete her. It was He in Mom and Ellen who had caught her attention.

In the same way Chris's husband, Bruce, noted Christ in her, and he soon placed his faith in Him.

And the children noted the change in Chris and Bruce: a son gave his life to Christ, the daughter, then a second son.

Then there was Gene.

It was a Friday night in mid-January and the temperature was at -38°F. Snow had smothered everything outdoors.

Gene was reading *Mere Christianity* by C. S. Lewis, a gift to him from one of my Christian friends. I had not yet read it. Fifty or sixty pages into the book, Gene laid it on the living room carpet and said, "That blasted Lewis went along fine until he changed tacks."

"In what way?"

"Lewis started out logical. I expected he would continue. He proved God's existence, but he took a leap into faith when it came to Christianity. He didn't even attempt to logically prove Christ's supposed position as Son of God and Savior."

"He couldn't, because Christianity is based on faith not proof, although it's all true."

"I can't accept something on blind faith. That's unrealistic. It bothers me that people do."

"It must be pretty important to you or you wouldn't be so worked up."

"I'm not worked up. It's not important," he said, and lighted a cigarette and took a quick drag, a usual practice when he was bothered.

In the six months of my Christianity, we had had so many similar conversations that this one did not seem unique. As far as I could see, Gene was still anti-Christian. And in the morning when I saw *Mere Christianity* on the carpet, I picked it up, closed it, and put it on the coffee table with some regret, for I had hoped God would touch Gene's spirit through the book. My friend had thought it possible, since Lewis was as logical as Gene.

After lunch Gene took his coffee to the living room and I followed. He arranged himself in his chair with his knees carefully crossed, and said, "I'd like to go to church with you tomorrow."

"You what?" I said in total surprise.

His eyes met mine and they were dead serious. "I'd like to go with you—"

"Because—"

"Because I'm a Christian."

I was so in wonder that I could only whisper, "A Christian?"

"Yes."

Frost clouded the glass doors and hid the balcony and the street. With no details to distract, I focused totally on Gene. Maybe that was why I heard the emotion behind his quiet yes and saw the light that came to his eyes with the affirmation.

"What happened?" I said, fully regaining my voice, but keeping the same wonder. "Last I knew, Lewis's jump into faith upset you."

"It did, but I couldn't seem to forget the matter. And this morning I started to wonder why I thought I could approach Christianity through logic, when Lewis, who had a finer mind than mine, couldn't."

"Then, you've been trying to approach Christianity?"

"I guess so, but I didn't fully know it. Anyhow, it occurred to me that I must either accept Christ by faith, or deny Him."

He set his coffee cup on the floor and continued. "After that I found myself thinking about my self-sufficiency, my ability to handle anything that came along without anyone's help—not even God's. I saw that I was believing in self to the exclusion of God." Gene had been speaking quietly. He now said humbly, "I saw my pride, and I wanted to change. I wanted to rely on God. I asked Christ to forgive me and head up my life."

I nodded, too moved to comment. Gene stood, came to me on the couch, and put his arms around me. "It wasn't just the book that influenced me," he said. "It was Douglas' signs and you—the change in you. You're happier."

At that moment I understood Gene's role in my salvation. "Mainly, it was you who led me to Christ," I said. "I don't think I could've understood His love if it weren't for yours."

Gene gave me a long kiss, as if expressing that, through God, we were joined body, soul and spirit—and we would never be separated from love again.

I didn't think we would. For the same love and appreciation I had felt on the drive home from the Riviera had been with me and was still with me—it would be forever. I didn't analyze that conclusion; six months of loving Gene had made it a fact.

When I told Douglas that his father was a Christian, his eyes filled with pleasure.

"Dad told me it was partly because of your signs," I said.

Douglas' eyes widened to hold even more joy and he ran off and took down the tape strips.

CHAPTER XXIII

That February morning when I drove to Fran's, I noticed the depth of the last night's fall of snow only because the sun came down strong, laying a hard shine on it. My mind was on her. Just yesterday she had been notified that in a few days there would be a child welfare hearing at which a judge would decide whether Eddie would be returned to her. In the six months of Eddie's absence, she had been drunk eighty percent of the time; thus she feared the court would remove him permanently. These last twenty-four hours she had been nervously pacing the house, trying to stay sober for the hearing, trying to ignore Archie, who was heaped over the kitchen table, urging her to join him in a drink.

Though I was taking her to the hearing, I wouldn't be allowed in the courtroom. But I knew it wasn't a human she needed in there; it was Christ. I also felt that God wanted me to tell her His plan of salvation. Even though I had done so a few months ago and she had angrily rejected it, He wanted me to tell her again.

But I doubted she would listen. When she was set against something, she stayed set.

I parked and walked across the porch. She let me in and motioned me to her couch. From there I had a view of the kitchen table and noted that Archie wasn't at his usual spot. "Where's Archie?" I asked.

"In there," she said, pointing at the bedroom door on the opposite wall.

"Is he asleep?"

"He's passed out. He just finished a quart of wine. I'm worried about him. He's been vomiting blood."

"My dad does that."

"From drinking?"

"Yes. It's an ulcer in his esophagus. Archie should see a doctor."

"He won't. He hates them. The last time he was in the hospital, they kicked him out because he was drinking mouthwash."

"Why was he drinking mouthwash?"

"Because he needed a drink," she said, moving toward the kitchen. "Do you want coffee?"

"Yes."

Soon she came back with the coffee. She sat at the other end of the couch, sipped her coffee, and nervously rubbed her finger against her thumbnail—the hearing evidently was on her mind.

"The hearing?" I said.

She nodded. "I've got to get Eddie back."

In her love that seemed best. But I thought about Eddie running on the street and jumping on the bed while she and Archie were passed out, and it didn't seem for the best to me. But with her need for him, I hated to think that.

"I'm scared," she said.

"I wish I could be in court. I know I can't, but I wish you'd let Jesus be with you."

"Why would He go? What's He ever done for me? Where was He when they took Eddie away?"

"He loves you."

"Some love He's got. I don't want it."

Even though the line of her jaw and spine went rigid, I started to explain God's redemptive plan. Oddly, she didn't interrupt, as I expected she would. And after a while I noted that her eyes were attentively on me. Then as I finished the last word, God touched her. I saw it happen. The rigid line of her spine broke. Her jutting chin pulled back. Her eyes warmed.

I said, "Would you like to give Jesus your life and quit disobeying Him?"

"Yes," she whispered, lowering her head.

I remembered that after testifying, Laurie had walked

around her glass coffee table and knelt before me with her hands in mine. Now I went to Fran and knelt and took her hands. "Just repeat after me," I said. "I'm sorry for my sins, Jesus."

"I'm sorry for my sins, Jesus."

"Forgive my sins."

"Forgive my sins."

"I give You my life."

"I give You my life."

"Amen."

"Amen."

"That makes us sisters," I said.

"Sisters?"

"Sisters in Christ."

"Sisters in Christ," she said gently, obviously pleased that we were sisters.

Rather than stand, I stayed on my knees, thinking: *She won't drink now. With Christ heading her life, she'll stay sober and she'll take good care of Eddie—if he comes home.* I said, "Maybe we should pray about the hearing."

With her head low she said, "Please bring Eddie back home."

We arrived several minutes before the hearing and sat in a small waiting room. The door to the courtroom was on our left. I picked up a magazine and leafed through without pausing to stop and read. As if to give herself an extra measure of security, Fran kept on her purple ski jacket with the belt buckled. She picked up a magazine, but instead of opening it, she took a tissue from her jacket and began twining and untwining it around her finger. She played with the tissue until it shredded, then stuffed it into her pocket. "What time is it?" she said.

"I don't know. I didn't wear my watch."

"It must be about time."

I glanced at the door. "It must be."

Fran found another tissue and wound it around her finger. Finally, when that tissue fell apart, the door opened and a tight-faced woman in a crisp, pink dress called Fran in.

I returned my magazine to the white table. I watched the door and silently prayed that God would move the judge to give Eddie back to Fran. *He belongs with his mother. Surely that would be right, Lord.* Finally the door opened and Fran came out.

"What happened?" I said, unable to read her eyes, which were as black and blank as the door shutting behind her.

But a second later her eyes lighted up and she said, "The judge is giving Eddie to me."

"He is? Is he really?"

"God answered my prayer," she said.

"When can Eddie come?"

"In three months. It's a probation. The judge says if I stay sober for three months, then Eddie can come home." She added in a quiet but firm voice, "I'm going to make it."

Tears came as I said, "I know you'll make it."

We celebrated. We went to a restaurant and had coffee, hamburgers and french fries in gravy. Though we had spent many hours talking, this was the first time that we had laughed together.

Fran stayed sober, and two weeks after the court hearing, she entered an educational program sponsored by Canada Manpower for adults who had not completed grade 10. After she completed that course of study, she planned to learn how to type. "Typists earn good money," she told me. "I could support Eddie. I could take care of all the kids."

I could see her future: Archie sobering up, her typing, him roofing, him becoming a Christian, them marrying, all the children at home.

Besides attending school, she began to read her Bible daily and to attend Bible study with me occasionally. Then one night, several weeks after she had started school, she served me coffee at her kitchen table and opened her Bible. "I like this," she said. "I read it last night." She then read: " 'A new commandment I give unto you, That ye love one another; as I have loved you, that ye also love one another. By this shall all men know that ye are my disciples, if ye have love one to another' " (John 13:34-35).

Fran said, "It means that God wants me to love other people."

To see Fran want to love others was to see God, and I cried.

The next night I was sitting at her kitchen table. Archie

had just struggled up from his chair and said, "I'll give you girls your privacy."

Even though the Lord had told me to simply love Fran, I was worried and I felt I must give her advice. "Why don't you ask him to leave?"

"I told you I can't."

"I guess I don't understand. He wants you to drink with him. I've heard him offer you drinks. Why take the chance? Why put yourself under that kind of temptation? It won't be long until the probation's over. You've almost made it."

"I love him," she said. "I can't kick him out."

"I don't understand."

"I can't . . ." And she changed the subject to school.

Then on a late afternoon in May under a sky that was as gray as a robin's wing, I walked to Fran's door. It was three days before the probation would be over. The door was half-way open. I knocked and waited a few minutes, thinking that the door shouldn't be open, yet almost knowing why it was. No one came, no sound came from the house. With a sinking feeling, I pushed open the door and walked into the dusty living room and toward the kitchen.

The kitchen lights were out, but by the time I got to the archway, my eyes had adjusted to the dim light. I stopped there. Archie was at one end of the table and Fran at the other. She was a shadow. Her neck was a gray column, wavering under the support of a bone of jelly. Her hair was black yarn. I smelled sweet, spicy wine.

She didn't see me, and I gazed at her as I might at a film. *This isn't real,* I thought. *This isn't my friend Fran. This doesn't mean she'll lose Eddie.* I felt cold and sick. I must have rocked forward, for the board under my foot creaked. Before she could glance up and see me, I spun around and flew through the living room and out the door.

I tore to the car and sank against the seat and cried out to God. "How could she drink? You gave her the chance to have Eddie and she threw it away."

For a minute I couldn't think, then it seemed I must save Fran. I must go in, sober her up, evict Archie, and call Social Welfare and explain that this was just a small slip. Archie was behind it; but now that he was gone, couldn't they overlook it? Or maybe Social Welfare was unaware of the drinking. In that case I could sober her up and no one would be the wiser.

No, you can't, I thought, and I listened, for it seemed to be God.

Then what should I do?

Love her.

Just that?

Yes.

All right, Lord, but I don't understand.

Over the next couple of days I understood some of God's meaning. Fran had chosen her will over God's, and neither I nor any human could set matters straight for her. Eddie's situation was between her and God—and I had to leave it there. But God was giving me an opportunity to love Fran—despite what looked like a future of Archie and drinking, to accept her as she was, to love her as I had not loved Bonnie and Carla and Gene.

I didn't hear from Fran until the night that the probation would have been over and Eddie would have been returned. She phoned. Her voice was so thick with whatever she was drinking that I had to strain to make out her words. "I'm at Rita's. Her sister won't give us five dollars for a drink. Rita said she'd kick her teeth in if she didn't. Rita's sister said if Rita kicked her, she'd call the police."

Fran paused. "Rita's sister . . ." Then a long pause. "I've lost Eddie."

"I know."

"I don't think Welfare will ever give him back."

"I don't know."

"Muriel . . ."

"Yes?"

"Are we still sisters?"

My logic insisted *no*. But there came the murmur of a higher logic. Fran was drunk, but in her heart she knew how wrong she'd been. She did want to follow Jesus, to obey Him. It would be only a matter of time, I was certain, before she would allow Him to free her from the dungeon of alcohol.

"Fran, we'll always be sisters."

CHAPTER XXIV

I hung up. Though I should have gone to the kitchen where Gene was wrist deep in ten pounds of hamburger for a church dinner meatloaf, I couldn't. Fran's loss was too much mine; I had to let my hurt settle. *Dear Lord,* I thought, *what do I pray?* There seemed just one possible prayer and I silently said it: *I give You every plan I've made for Fran's life. I accept Your will in her life—whatever that may be.*

I then went to the kitchen. Gene was lifting his hands from the meatloaf mix and I asked, "Is it all mixed?"

He nodded, rinsed his hands in the sink, then asked, "Who called?"

"Fran."

"What did she want?"

"She's upset. Today's the day she would have gotten Eddie back."

"I'm sorry she didn't, but she brought it on herself."

"You can't say that. You don't know what you'd have done in her circumstances. She misses her kids. Archie drinks. She was tempted."

"Any sane person would have booted him out."

"Maybe she was afraid of being alone."

"She'd have been alone only until Eddie came home."

I took out several 9 x 13 pans, then said, "I know you don't like her, but I would think you'd be feeling some compassion."

"She doesn't need compassion. She needs someone to put some sense in her." Then, evidently realizing that his antagonism outdistanced the occasion, he said, "Look, I wish her the best. I hope she makes it someday."

Perhaps I had a hurt look in my eyes which gave him further insight, for he said, "Forgive me, gal. I'm sure this has got you down."

I nodded.

"If there's ever anything I could do, let me know."

"I will."

"I do mean that."

"I know you do."

That was Thursday and I loved Gene, as I had now these eleven months of my Christianity. But on Monday while he was at work, my mood started to shift. At first I thought it was the sun I disliked, the heavy square of it on the living room carpet. I shut the draperies, a little surprised. Normally I loved the sun, and just yesterday I had been looking forward to the end of June; then it would be up nineteen hours, and so slimly beneath the horizon the other five that the night would be as gray as dawn. Later when I vacuumed the bedroom and saw Gene's dirty socks beside a leg of the dresser, I gave them a grim look and felt unfriendly toward him.

When he came home from work, I went to the hall while he set his hard hat on the closet shelf; I realized that I couldn't stand him. While he pulled off his safety shoes, which were actually cowboy boots with hard toes, I thought: *If he had any taste at all, he'd wear ordinary work boots, not pretentious cowboy boots.* I noted the angry boil on his forehead, which anyone with any suavity would have covered with a Band-Aid. I saw his rough face. His watery blue eyes. "Hi, gal," he said in the voice of a milksop.

He reached for me and I stepped back into the living room. "I'm not in the mood," I said.

"I thought you were over that kind of thing."

"I'm not in any kind of thing. I'm just not in the mood for that."

"For just a kiss?"

"Forget it," I said. "I don't want to talk about it."

In his condescending way, he went to his gold-striped chair and read the newspaper. Any man who was a man would have pursued the matter, overcome me with his boldness, and made me love him. Doubts flared in my head. *Why did I rush into marriage with an old maid like him? I should have waited for a flamboyant man to come along.* I hurried from him to the kitchen. I pulled out the electric frying pan, plugged it in, and unwrapped a package of hamburger.

"Need any help?" Gene called.

My irritation almost became anger at his attempt to be friendly. Couldn't he see I wanted my privacy? "No," I said.

"What are we having?"

"Hamburgers." I started slapping together the patties.

"We're almost finished with construction," he said.

I dreaded leaving Fran, my friends, the church, the Bible studies. In my concern over going, I forgot my dislike of him and went to the living room. "When will you be done? Have you got the date?"

"Not exactly, but it'll probably be in the first week of August. We should be putting out pulp by then."

"Won't they need you after that? What if there's a problem?"

"I'm leaving one of my engineers."

"I'm not anxious to go."

"You should be. You can get back into real estate."

"I guess so, but that doesn't make me want to leave this."

For a minute I had forgotten his beacon boil and rough face, but they now came back to full view and I gave him a cold look.

"What's wrong with you?" he said.

"Nothing. I'm just preoccupied."

"I don't think so. I think you're getting back to the way you used to be."

"I'm not. I'm simply thinking about many things."

"Like what?"

"Nothing," I said and turned. "I've got to put on the hamburgers."

Gene followed me to the frying pan. "You've read Ephesians on marriage?" (Eph. 5:22-33)

"Yes."

"Maybe you'd better read it again."

"Maybe you're the one who needs to read it. It's the way you are that makes me feel the way I do. If you'd change, I wouldn't feel like this," I said.

I heard myself and I thought, *Oh, no, Lord—what am I doing?*

"I'm sorry," I said. "I don't know why I'm acting like this. Forgive me."

He nodded. "But think before you take off like that again. Think a little what it does to me."

"I don't want to hurt you. I meant what I told you a while back. I'm trying to change."

"I know, gal," he said along with a glance at the frying pan. "The light's red. Do you want the hamburgers in?"

"I'll do it," I said, wanting some time to think. "Finish your paper."

He left. Though with my apology my thoughts about his boil had receded, and his manner had assumed the authority necessary to manage the construction of a pulp mill, yet I felt no love for him. Rather, I felt neutral. I was very upset with myself.

Almost in tears, I put the hamburgers in the frying pan and thought: *What's wrong with me, Lord? How can I turn from loving to detesting without any provocation? Where does that kind of animosity come from?*

I answered the last question by thinking it came from the rub of our personalities, a case of the sail against the anchor. *But that can't be,* I thought, remembering that while driving home from the Riviera Motel, I had appreciated our differences.

Then I found my thoughts going back to my childhood with an alcoholic father, an alcoholic mother, the alcoholic aunts, uncles, friends. I felt the trauma of then—not knowing from one day to the next whether I was coming home from school to a mother making a pie or a mother making a drink. Or to a father eager for a game of Ping-Pong or for a talk about good Old Henry and the peanut butter sandwiches they had eaten during the Depression.

Something within the trauma brought out the cold feelings toward Gene.

Though I had no conscious reason, I shied from discovering what specifics in each relationship had harmed me. Somehow I knew that would be destructive. The important fact was the knowledge of the origin of the coldness.

While I finished fixing dinner, I had a strong impression that I should pray for each of the people who had harmed me. "Lord," I whispered, "forgive them. Bless them. Show them the same mercy You've shown me."

I felt more free. Would I now be able to love Gene?

I thought it possible. And I thought I knew the method.

In bed that night I said to Gene, "You still know I'm sorry?"

The draperies were not completely pulled, and with the touch of a streetlight on the bed I could make out his profile —his Roman nose, high forehead, curly hair, the movement of his mouth as he said, "Yes."

"I think I know how to learn to love you."

"How?"

"By studying love in the Bible." Because I seldom talked about love, I was shy about continuing and faltered a little as I finished. "I'm pretty sure I know why I get cold toward you, but I think I'm getting over it."

"What causes it?"

"It's from being the child of alcoholics."

"I don't know. My mom didn't drink; my dad drank but he never got drunk—I wasn't raised like you. But if you think so, it probably is."

"I hope the kids won't be like me. I hope they can love."

"They will."

"You don't know that."

"Don't project. What good does that do?"

"You're right. I shouldn't."

Neither of us spoke, and I thought Gene had gone to sleep. Then I saw his eyes were open, gazing toward the dresser beyond the foot of the bed.

"Aren't you tired?" I asked.

"No, gal," he said, reaching around to my shoulder and pulling me to him.

"Not now," I said, my feelings still as neutral as they had been in the kitchen.

He breathed out hard in exasperation. "What have you just been telling me?"

"I've been stating what I'm going to be doing."

"And you can't start now?"

"No."

"I totally do not understand you," he said, and flipped to his side.

That week, with the aid of a Bible concordance, I studied love.

Then around ten o'clock on Friday night, while Gene

watched television, I went to the bedroom and looked up a few of the scriptures I had found.

Those defining love:

"Love worketh no ill to his neighbour: therefore love is the fulfilling of the law" (Rom. 13:10).

"Beloved, let us love one another: for love is of God; and every one that loveth is born of God, and knoweth God. He that loveth not knoweth not God; for God is love" (1 John 4:7-8).

"Love is patient and kind; it is not jealous or conceited or proud; love is not ill-mannered or selfish or irritable; love does not keep a record of wrongs; love is not happy with evil, but is happy with the truth. Love never gives up; and its faith, hope, and patience never fail. Love is eternal. . ." (1 Cor. 13:4-8, GNB).

Those showing how to have love:

"And above all these things *put on* charity [love], which is the bond of perfectness" (Col. 3:14).

". . . strive for righteousness, faith, love, and peace, together with those who with a pure heart call out to the Lord for help" (2 Tim. 2:22, GNB).

"My little children, let us not love in word, neither in tongue; but in deed and in truth" (1 John 3:18).

I laid down my Bible, believing that I finally understood the nature of love. I remembered that once I would have given my real estate career and the colonial for a feeling of love.

But loving was more than having feelings of sensuality and appreciation and pride for Gene. It was partly, as I had once momentarily realized, turning my attention from myself to him. But beyond that, it was going on and choosing to love him, practicing love for him, putting on love despite cold feelings.

It was setting my mind toward God and Gene. And then I would have that which was God and eternal. That which Gene had given me. That which I had given Fran.

I had to go to him—now.

But I didn't find him in the family room watching television or in the living room. Douglas' bedroom light was on, and I walked in and asked, "Where's Dad?"

"Mr. Powell came for him."

"Why?"

"His car needed a jump."

"When did Dad leave?"

"A while ago."

"How long does it take to jump a car?"

"A while," Douglas said distractedly, giving his attention to two short lengths of wire that he was looping together.

Beside him lay a coat hanger with a length missing. Because he often made puzzles from coat hangers, I asked, "Is that a puzzle?"

"Yes."

"You'll have to finish it tomorrow. It's late."

"But I'm busy."

"Tomorrow, Douglas."

He got into bed; I kissed him, turned out the light, and went to the living room couch, which faced the front door. *Hurry up, Gene,* I thought. But chances were he would be on the long side of a while. Earl Powell was a talker and was bound to be chatting on some subject long after the car was started. I had mixed feelings: excitement, a little like that before a date with a loved boyfriend; shyness, the same shyness I had felt when I told Gene I would be studying love in the Bible.

Because of the shy feeling, I considered turning off the lamp beside the couch so that I could say what I had to say in the dark. But I left it on; the secrecy of the dark might veil what I would be saying.

After about fifteen minutes Gene came through the front door and set a flashlight on the shelf beside his hard hat. His hands were greasy and his T-shirt smudged.

"Douglas told me where you were. You look like you had to do more than just jump Earl's car."

"I did. He had corroded battery terminals." Gene walked to the kitchen, turned on the water, and started to lather his hands. "Cleaning a battery's a simple matter, but Earl knows nothing about cars."

"You've got grease on your shirt," I said.

"I'll be changing for bed in a minute," he said and rinsed his hands, then reached for the towel on the handle of the refrigerator. "I thought you were down for the night."

"I was, but something came up."

"With the kids?"

"No." Though this would be difficult, I thought it best to go straight to it. "I've finished studying the scriptures on love."

I paused. It took some effort to look directly at him, but I did. "I've learned what love is. I know how to have it. Will you understand what I mean if I say, I *will* love you?"

Maybe he didn't quite understand my meaning, for at first he just nodded and gave me a faint smile. But after a moment his entire face lighted up and he had me in his arms and I felt the beat of his heart against my forehead. I put my arms around his neck, placed a hand on his hair, and lifted my face to his.

"I do love you," I said.